REVIVAL

God Will Come to Where You Are

Antonio M. Palmer

REVIVAL – God Will Come to Where You Are

Copyright © 2018 by Antonio M. Palmer

All rights reserved. No part of this book may be reproduced in any form, stored in a retrieved system, or in any form by any means – electronic, mechanical, photocopy, recording, or otherwise – without prior written permission of the publisher, except as provided by United States of America copyright law.

Unless otherwise indicated, all Scripture quotations are from the King James Version of the Holy Bible. Scripture quotations noted NKJV are from the New King James Version, copyright © 1979, 1980, 1982 by Thomas Nelson, Inc. Publishers. Scripture quotations noted NASB are from the New American Standard Bible®, copyright © the Lockman Foundation 1960, 1962, 1963, 1968, 1971, 1972, 1973, 1975, 1977. Used by permission.

ISBN 978-1-947741-29-4

Published by Kingdom Publishing, LLC
Odenton, Maryland 21113
www.kingdompublishingllc.com

Printed in the U.S.A.

I dedicate this book to all of the prayer warriors worldwide who do not relent in the pursuit of God's presence.

Acknowledgments

I'd like to thank the love of my life, my beautiful wife and best friend, Pastor Barbara Palmer, for praying for me every day and giving me joy while challenging me to be the best man I can be in Christ. Thanks for pursuing destiny together.

I'd like to also thank my church family, Kingdom Celebration Center and Kingdom Alliance of Churches, International. You guys truly desire God and I'm glad to experience an open heaven with you.

I'd like to thank Prophet Delavago and Pastor Aretha Scruggs for your daily prayers, words of wisdom and using your prophetic gift to herald the sound of Revival. You guys make me feel like I can do anything.

I'd like to thank my son, Minister Randy Curtis, Jr., my daughter-in-law, Kimberly, and OHOP (Odenton House of Prayer) for praying for Revival and setting the standard of pursuing a holy God. I'm compelled to chase harder after *Yeshua* because of you.

Table of Contents

Chapter One: **Revival is Coming!** 1

Chapter Two: **The Prophets are Prophesying - The Lord is Coming!** 7

Chapter Three: **Revival by the River** 13

Chapter Four: **Repent** 19

Chapter Five: **Let in the Light** 25

Chapter Six: **How to Know if God is Calling You to Revival** 33

Chapter Seven: **His Name is Jealous** 45

Chapter Eight: **Draw Near to God** 53

Chapter Nine: **Diligently Seek Him** 65

Chapter Ten: **Cry Out!** 75

Chapter Eleven: **The Sound that Pleases God** 87

Chapter Twelve: **Fulfilling the Burden of Revival** 101

Chapter One

Revival is Coming!

The topic of revival is emerging like never before among the church world. People are sensing that God wants to do something in the earth. I don't know about you, but I don't want to miss out on what He is desiring to do in this season. It feels like the Lord is fluttering over His earth like when He first created it. Things are dark, chaotic and empty. Violence is more prevalent and hearts are failing for fear and love has waxed cold. We know the world is paying no attention to God, but it appears the church isn't either. However, like in other strategic times in history, Yahweh has a remnant that is sensing His coming to refresh the church and advance His kingdom. It's a divine setup. I am convinced that Revival is on the way and therefore am posturing myself to receive of Him. If you're sensing the same thing, then this book is definitely for you. Yeshua (Jesus) has given me keys for those who are being called to usher in the next move of God. In your hand are kingdom keys that will open the heavens over your life, your church and your city.

REVIVAL DEFINED

In many mainline denominations, revival used to carry the meaning of a special three-day service. An evangelist or preacher with the gift to enliven the people would be booked for those days to set the church ablaze, along with special choirs, praise teams and singers. If the services were really good, the pastor may extend it from three days to a full week! Admittedly, I would have a great time and feel good about having attended these services, feeling somewhat refreshed.

However, the kind of revival I want to refer to in this book carries a much different meaning; a meaning that supersedes a three-day refreshing or feel-good service. I like how Adrian Rogers of Love Worth Finding defines revival. He says it is "when God comes down."[1] He uses Isaiah 64:1 as his guide.

---

[1] Adrian Rogers, What Is Revival? When God Shows Up!
https://www.oneplace.com/ministries/love-worth-finding/read/articles/what-is-revival-when-god-shows-up-15645.html

Chapter One - Revival is Coming!

"Oh, that you [Almighty God] would rend the heavens, that you would come down, that the mountains might shake at Your presence" (Isaiah 64:1).

Dr. James Goll of Bethel Church in Redding, Pennsylvania and others have used this scripture to pinpoint the definition of revival. Dr. Rogers goes on to encourage us that revival – God coming down – is not impossible but highly possible and that it is inevitable. Like the Israelites (God's people) who were carried away into captivity, the Church is in a captive state bound by worldliness, complacency, lukewarmness and compromise. We are depleted and powerless. We need a sovereign move of God to shift the dynamics of our world. Satan seems to be getting the best of God's people and at this point only God can help us in our condition. We need God to come down! We need Him to revive us again.

Paul J. Bucknell says that revival is *"when God decides to change history to further the advance of His kingdom."*[2]

How can we get God to come down to where we are and change our world? Can a body of believers persuade the Creator, the Father of lights, to move on their behalf, to revive their homes, their church, their city, their nation? If so, what is it that they must do to make this happen? I pray that this book will light a match that ignites the flames of desperation and discipline

---

[2] www.foundationsforfreedom.net/Topics/Revival/Revival00.html

which ultimately causes our God to rend the heavens and come down.

One of the key elements of revival is sensing that God has initiated the first move by making you aware of the need for His presence. J. I. Packer says, *"Revival is God touching minds and hearts in an arresting, devastating, exalting way, to draw them to himself through working from the inside out rather than from the outside in."*[3] God arrests your attention. He makes you aware. This awareness becomes more demonstrative and breaks through your usual thought patterns – to the point where you are thinking of God and the need of Him more than you have ever done before. Know that this is the working of the Holy Spirit. You have become the candidate of His choosing for a location where He came come fulfill His desire of reviving His church and advancing His kingdom on Earth. He is looking for your, "Yes." God desires to use you and your church to facilitate miracles, healings, deliverance and salvation in your region in an unprecedented way. It is time you clear your throat so that you can vociferate the same burning cry unto the Lord, *"Oh that You would rend the heavens and come down!"* You will get God to come down to where you are.

Beloved, you are not alone. God is arresting many hearts and making them aware of the need of His presence. This is why I am inspired to write this book and to share valuable biblically-based ways that the Lord gave me; that every revivalist,

---

[3] J.I. Packer, "The Glory of God and the Reviving of Religion" in A God-Entranced Vision of All Things (pp. 100-104)

Chapter One - Revival is Coming!

every heart-arrested believer and intercessor needs in getting the Lord to *rend the heavens and come to where we are*. The ways or disciplines are not anything new. They just need to be put into practice intensely and consistently. It is what the Lord has already prescribed in His word. We have built programs and ministries, conferences and seminars around church growth while basically avoiding what God has already said we should do in order to have His nearness, His manifest presence in our lives. Nations were changed by the power of God, not by the will of man. Our greatest efforts, our most creative ideas and our political stance will not change our nation. It's going to take nothing less than the power of God. We need God to come down! We need Revival!

Chapter Two

The Prophets are Prophesying – "The Lord is Coming!"

One of the greatest revivals that ever took place was during the time of Herod, the king of Judaea. God's people were in a state of spiritual decline. The leaders of the people were self-righteous and instituted their traditions and oral teachings above the word of God. They were adding strenuous laws onto the original Torah which left the people bound and burdensome. They cared more about the revenues and profits of the Temple sacrifices than the condition of the people who were making the sacrifices. The Temple was no longer a house of prayer but a den of thieves. Diseases plagued the land and many were vexed with demonic possessions. On top of this, they were under the control of a godless government. The cultural climate of Israel was at an all-time low. Does this sound familiar? When there's a striking resemblance in your world to this, then it is ripe for revival.

PROPHETS WILL PROPHESY

We are told that God does nothing until He reveals it to His prophets (Amos 3:7). Before revival takes place the Lord will disclose it to His prophets so that they can sound the alarm. When the Lord was ready to change the environment of Israel and to relieve them of their suffering, He sent prophets to announce His coming.

There was an 84 year old, widowed woman who had gotten married in her early years of living. Her husband had died around seven years after they had married. She decided not to marry the rest of her life and dedicate her life to serving in the temple. Her name was Anna. She did not depart from the temple, but served God with fastings and prayers night and day. Anna was also a prophetess. We know that she was declaring the Messiah was coming, because Yeshua (Jesus) was presented in the temple and she immediately gave thanks unto the Lord and spoke concerning who He was to all that were looking for the redemption of Jerusalem (Luke 2:36-38).
God also revealed His coming to a devout and just man named Simeon. He was "waiting for the consolation of Israel" (Luke 2:25). In fact the Holy Ghost revealed to him that he wasn't going to die until he had seen the Messiah (v. 26). When he

walked into the temple and saw the baby, Jesus, he took him up in his arms and blessed God and began to prophesy and declare who Jesus was. He was even ready to go in peace because he had now laid eyes on the Son of God (v. 29-30). God had come to Earth to change the climate of Israel. Prophets were prophesying the brooding of revival. Many were catching onto the declaration of the prophets insomuch that Herod got wind of it and wanted to stop the pending revival. He practically did the same thing the Pharaoh had done in Egypt during the time of Moses by killing every Hebrew child two years old and younger. God's plan prevailed as the Christ-child was led into Africa for safety until Herod's death. A word of precaution – when the enemy hears the prophets declaring revival he believes it and will attempt to hinder it.

YAHWEH IS GRACIOUS

Simultaneous to the events of the Messiah's birth was the miraculous birth of his cousin. Many know him as the Baptizer, but Jesus declared him to be the greatest of all prophets (Luke 7:28). Being born of righteous parents well stricken in age who were also foretold of his prophetic assignment, this child was not the kind of child who could fit in with the other kids. I'm sure he was overly protected by his father Zacharias (a priest) and his mother Elizabeth who was born of the priestly lineage of Aaron. The events surrounding his birth were unusual. First, they couldn't have any children and there weren't any In Vitro Fertilization procedures 2000 years ago. Then there was the angelic announcement of his name. I'm sure Zacharias wanted to name the boy after himself – Zach, Jr. or little Zachary, but the Father had already chosen his name before he would be formed in his mother's womb. He gave him a name uncommon to any of his kinfolk. His name was so important that the angel, Gabriel, who appeared to Zacharias, summoned muteness upon his mouth until the child was born. Now, I've heard of daddies passing out at the birthing of their child, but never in history was there any other daddy made speechless at the prophetic announcement of having a child.

It was customary that on the eighth day after his birth, the day of circumcision for the male child, that the Hebrews would also name their child. Everyone was calling him Zacharias, after his father, but his mama wasn't having it. She corrected them and told them his actual name. They didn't take her word for it and acted as though they needed confirmation from the father, especially since they'd never heard a name like his ever among their kinfolk. The speechless father then took a writing tablet and scribbled upon it the name of his son – Y-O-C-H-A-N-A-N! And immediately upon holding up that tablet with those Hebrew letters spelling out the prophet's name, Zacharias' tongue was loosed and he could speak again. Well, after 9 months of not being able to talk, he did more than speaking; he broke out in praise and began singing under the power of the Holy Ghost! (Luke 1:57-80).

Yochanan (or John), not only had a unique name but he also was given an extraordinary assignment. It was to prepare the people for the coming of the Lord (Luke 1:16-17). Now we see

Chapter Two - The Prophets are Prophesying - The Lord is Coming!

why the Lord wanted his name to be Yochanan, which means "Yahweh is gracious." Grace always precedes revival. Yochanan's birth signified a season of grace where God was willing to do something special for His people that they did not deserve and they couldn't do on their own. He was ready to reconcile them unto Himself. Revival is a God-decision. I believe that He has decided again to come and do something in the earth for His people even in our present condition where we don't deserve His favor. The message of the Lord's grace will always be one of repentance. Repentance is a forerunner for revival.

LISTEN TO THE PROPHETS

The reason why I know that Revival is forthcoming is because various prophets are prophesying that the Lord is coming to awaken His people and to revive the church. Many prophets are declaring that the heavens are open and that a new season has begun. They are sounding the alarm of repentance, forgiveness and cleansing. The shofar is being blown and prophets are not sparing but crying aloud for the church to come out of lukewarmness and return to God. You must listen to the voice of the prophets today. The Spirit of God is speaking to the church. He that hath an ear, let him hear what the Spirit saith unto the church" (Revelation 2:7, 11, 17, 29; 3:6, 13, 22). You cannot afford to miss it this time. The presence of the Lord is coming in an unprecedented way and you can be very instrumental in ushering in His glory in your city. It will happen, with or without you. The prophets are prophesying!

"Believe in the Lord your God, so shall ye be established; believe His prophets, so shall ye prosper."
(2 Chronicles 20:20)

Chapter Three

Revival by the River

Yochanan receives a word from the Lord and he begins his ministry from the wilderness of Judaea and throughout the country alongside the Jordan River. The news of Yochanan's ministry grew where people from all over Israel began to come to hear him preach. They were coming from Jerusalem, Judaea and all the region around Jordan (Matthew 3:5). The Father gave him a candid message to preach to the multitude. His message was "Repent ye: for the kingdom of heaven is at hand" (Matthew 3:2). This message was so compelling that multitudes were coming to him confessing their sins as he was baptizing them (Matthew 3:6). Revival had begun by the Jordan River.

HINDERING SPIRITS AT THE RIVER

When revival comes, unfortunately, only a remnant usually embraces it though it's made available for all. As revival is being launched there will be people who will come in the midst of it and be a hindrance with their skepticism and antagonistic ways. Most of the people who hinder revival are religious people, especially leaders.

As Yochanan was baptizing people, he could not help but to notice the Pharisees and Sadducees in attendance. How did he notice them? Besides their religious attire, I'm sure their disposition and demeanor were contrary to the disposition of those who were confessing their sins. They were not happy campers. They were the religious folk who arrogantly felt they were already close to God. They argued that they were children of Abraham, already blessed, and saw no need for the commotion of Yochanan's preaching and baptismal services.

We should know that while the message of grace and repentance is being preached during revival, that religious spirits must be confronted, reproved and preached against. Of course, it would stir the pot of evil plotting. The enemy is infuriated with preachers of good news; with revivalist preachers and prophets who declare repentance and grace.

Yochanan lifted up his voice and directed a word exclusively to the Pharisees and Sadducees, "You generation of vipers, who hath warned you to flee from the wrath to come? Bring forth therefore fruits meet (answerable) for repentance: and think not to say within yourselves, we have Abraham to our father: for I say unto you, that God is able of these stones to raise up children unto Abraham. The axe is laid unto the root of the trees: therefore every tree which bringeth not forth good fruit is hewn down, and cast into the fire" (Matthew 3:7-9).

How's that for a revival message? The churches are in the condition that they are in today because of religious leaders who feel entitled, full of pride, and are leading people to themselves and not to God. Yeshua really had a field day on them when He confronted them. He had to rebuke them throughout His entire ministry. They sought to destroy His ministry and kill Him just to save their own status, religious institutions and doctrines. Yeshua called them open graveyards! Now you cannot be any deadlier than that. We have open graveyard preachers and dead churches that refuse to let the Lord come to them.

OUTSIDE AUTHORITY

Yochanan's preaching not only hit the religious sector, but even political and governmental officials showed up at his revival services. Yochanan had reproved Herod the tetrarch for having an affair with his brother, Phillip's wife, Herodias and for all the other evils he had done (Luke 3:19). As a tetrarch, Herod governed a quarter of the country. I imagine Yochanan's rebuke of Herod circulated around the country. It would have been on every news channel in our day. Nothing spreads as fast as bad news. I also imagine that the news of this rebuke helped usher many people to Yochanan's baptismal services. What manner of man was this that he would rebuke a high ranking official? This news was too juicy to stay home. You had to go to Yochanan's services just in case he would say something else 'fly off the handle.' Yochanan's boldness to preach and to say what God tells him to say paved the way for souls to rush to his services.

Herod was so offended and angered with Yochanan that eventually he had him thrown in prison. But Yochanan knew he had to decrease while Yeshua's ministry increased. Yochanan was yielding to Yeshua – the preparatory, cleansing message of the prophet was giving way to the presence of the Lord. The one thing you don't want to do is see God show up and try to keep yourself elevated as though you are the reason why revival exist. Get out of the way when you see Yeshua come. Preacher, prophet, intercessor, prayer warrior, your only responsibility is to prepare the way for revival – the coming of Yeshua.

One more thing, Yochanan did not cower in the presence of anyone else in seats of authority. He did not change up his word and prophesy houses and land. He didn't try to hold a praise service when it was a service of repentance. Evidence of the primary stages of revival will always be people repenting and confessing their sins. Revival is not a feel good service, but its initial stage is always a time of awful reflection of the sins we have committed before a holy God. It is the duty of the prophets to get us there. This prepares people to receive the Messiah. This prepares people to receive salvation and others to

Chapter Three - Revival by the River

renew a stronger, more intimate relationship with the true and living God.

Chapter Four

Repent

When the Messiah shows up, He extends the message of grace that was preached by Yochanan, "Repent: for the kingdom of heaven is at hand" (Matthew 4:17). Repentance is the posture of the heart opened to receive the love poured out from above. This is a way that you can get God to come to where you are. When the Lord sees a heart in a penitent posture, He shows up. Repentance is not mere tears of sorrow. The Greek word that is used in the New Testament for repent is *metanoeo*. Metanoeo is a compound word. It is taken from two Greeks words, *"meta"* and *"noieo."* Meta means *"beyond or outside of."* Noieo means *"to perceive with the mind, to understand."* We can be safe to define metanoeo as *"taking one's mind/thoughts beyond and outside of its habituations (what it is accustomed to)."*[4] Thayer's Dictionary further defines metanoeo as *"a change of mind for better, heartily to amend with abhorrence of one's past sins."*[5]

Taking one's mind outside of what it is accustomed to thinking, believing, perceiving, etc. requires one important thing – a new revelation. There's no repentance without a revelation. You need something to help you change your mind. You will not wake up one day and just decide you're going to live for God. You need revelation. Revelation is a divine word proclaiming a spiritual reality. Its intent is to influence and persuade the heart and mind to yield to its truth.

The revelation that Yochanan presented was very new to the Hebrew multitude that came to hear him speak. He proclaimed that the kingdom of heaven was at hand. It was as near to them as the person that was standing next to them or the air that was brushing against their body. This was new to them because the religious authorities had pretty much disconnected the people from the reality of a God who is near to them.

The Pharisees had the bulk of the people thinking more about not breaking laws rather than being in relationship with the God of the laws. The people perceived their God only through the lens of laws and precepts which was mostly manmade and placed upon them by the self-righteous leaders who had no care for their souls.

---

[4] https://en.m.wikipedia.org/wiki/Metanoia_(theology)
[5] https://www.studylight.org/desk/interlinear.cgi?ref=39003002 – [Thayer's Dictionary]

Chapter Four - Repent

HEAVY LADEN

This way of thinking had them in a "heavy laden" condition. I rightfully used the term heavy laden because it carried the idea of loading someone with a burden of rites and unwarranted precepts. The Pharisees were putting people under such religious restraint by their unwarranted, manmade traditions that it made the actual word of God non effective (Mark 7:13). This is the term that the Messiah used just shortly after giving tribute to Yochanan the Baptizer and his prophetic ministry. He lifted up his voice after praying to the Father, "Come unto Me, all ye that labour and are *heavy laden,* and I will give you rest. Take my yoke upon you, and learn of Me; for I am meek and lowly in heart: and ye shall find rest unto your souls. For My yoke is easy and My burden is light" (Matthew 11:28-30).

The Pharisees weighed the people down with their unwarranted precepts and traditions. The people needed a new revelation to destroy their present way of thinking; to get them to think outside of what their minds were accustomed to. And they got that new revelation from the baptizing prophet, Yochanan, "Repent ye: for the kingdom of heaven is at hand."

There are so many people bound today by the yoke of religious influence and traditions that undermine effects of the word of God. We are so stuck on promoting self, living a successful life, going after our destiny, reaping material prosperity; so controlled by greed, lust and pride and cannot get out of it. We don't pray, we don't seek the face of the Lord, we don't study God's word, and we blame everything on being church hurt. Like the church of Sardis, we claim that we are alive but are dead (Revelation 3:1). We will not repent until we have a revelation of the nearness of the kingdom of God. We need intercessors to cry aloud, "Lord, come to where we are! Lord, come with a revelation that will change our minds, that will make us look upon our sins with abhorrence, that will make us wholeheartedly turn to You."

My friend, the spirit of Elijah and a John the Baptist-like word is going forth today and crying out for the church to repent. We are in a season where the kingdom of God is at hand. And we can get God to come to us when we receive this revelation and allow it to make us think beyond what our minds are used to thinking.

CONVINCING GOD

Is God convinced that we are convinced? How do we know if we've genuinely repented? Milton Crum defines metanoia (repentance) as "a change of perception with its behavioral fruit."[6] The fruit of repentance is not a tear. The fruit of repentance is behavioral not emotional. When you start thinking differently you will start acting differently. If you want to know if a church is in revival, don't look for miracles, but see if the people are acting differently. See if they are crying out to God. See if they are confessing their sins. See if their worship is

---

[6] https://en.m.wikipedia.org/wiki/Metanoia_(theology)

more intense. See if they discipline themselves to hear the word of God. See if they are reprioritizing their lives to be in His presence. Don't look for tears; look for a change of behavior. Yochanan preached, "Bring forth therefore fruits meet for repentance" (Matthew 3:8). If there is not a change in behavior, then there is not a true repentance. If there is no noticeable change in a person's life, then you can rest assure that God is not convinced that you wholeheartedly repented.

AUTHENTIC REPENTANCE

I love the example in the book of Acts. We have the account of Apostle Paul preaching in Ephesus. The power of God was so great that special miracles were demonstrated by Paul. He took handkerchiefs and aprons that were in his possession and sent them to the sick and they were being healed along with others being delivered from demon possession (Acts 19:11-12). Afterwards, seven sons of a Hebrew priest named Sceva attempted to cast evil spirits out of a man like Paul did and totally muffed. The evil spirits leaped out of the man and overpowered them. They made them flee out of the house naked and traumatized (v. 14-16).

News got around to all the Hebrews and Greeks of this incident and the name of the Lord, Yeshua, was greatly honored. Many people believed. The bible says they *"confessed* and *showed* their deeds"* (Acts 19:18). This first shows that they openly and willingly abhorred what they were in by doing something. They *showed* their deeds.

How did they show their deeds? The next verse gives us a great example of how deeds were shown. Many witches and diviners that were practicing witchcraft and sorcery, when they heard and received the revelation of Paul's preaching and heard what had happened to the sons of Sceva, were among those that believed (truly repented). They showed their deeds by bringing their magical books to the revival service and burned them in front of everybody. It was as simple as it may seem. This is why Luke recorded the value of these books that were burnt up – 50,000 pieces of silver. If these pieces of silver were denarii (a day's wage), then the estimated value would equal to approximately $5.5 million dollars today![7]

They didn't sell their books to unsaved witches; they burned them. They repented. They abhorred their evil practices. They had a change of heart due to the divine revelation they received. Revival will be marked by the abhorrence of evil deeds. Repentance is not just a feeling of sorrow but an abhorrence of the things that kept you from the life of God. You're not just sorry for your wrongdoings, but you have hatred toward them.

---

[7] https://www.quora.com/How-many-dollars-today-would-equal-50-000-silver-coins-in-the-book-of-Acts-19-19

Chapter Five

Let in the Light

Dutch Sheets explains in his book, Intercessory Prayer, that repentance is like letting in the light which is true revelation of Jesus. He uses the analogy of a camera to illustrate repentance:

> The word "light" in 2 Corinthians 4:4 is *photismos,* which means "illumination." It is similar to another word in Ephesians 1:18, "enlightened" which is the word *photizo* – "to let in light." We can almost see the English words "photo" or "photograph" in these Greek words; they are, indeed, derived from them. What

happens when one takes a photo? The shutter on the camera opens, letting in light, which brings an image. If the shutter on the camera does not open, there will be no image or picture, regardless of how beautiful the scenery or elaborate the setting.

The same is true in the souls of human beings. And this is exactly what is being said in these two verses in 2 Corinthians 4. It sounds like photography language. It makes no difference how glorious our Jesus or wonderful our message, if the veil (shutter) is not removed, there will be no true image (picture) of Christ. Oh, sometimes we talk people into a salvation prayer without a true revelation (unveiling), but there is usually no real change. That is why fewer than 10 percent – I've heard figures as low as 3 percent – of people who "get saved" in America become true followers of Christ. The reason is that there is no true biblical repentance, which only comes from biblical revelation.

Repentance does not mean to "turn and go another way" – a change of direction. That's the Greek word *epistrepho,* often translated *"converted"* or *"turn"* and is the result of repentance. Repentance – *metanoia* – means to have *"a new knowledge or understanding"* – a change of mind.

In biblical contexts repentance is a new understanding that comes from God through an unveiling (revelation). It is the reversing of the effects of the Fall through Adam. Humanity chose their own wisdom, their own knowledge of good and evil, right and wrong. Humanity now needs a new knowledge – from God. Paul said in Acts 26:18 he was called *"to open their eyes"* – enlightenment, unveiling, revelation, repentance – *"so that they may turn (epistrepho) from darkness to light."*[8]

There you have it. Repentance is a new understanding. It is the opening of the eyes of our understanding so that we may turn from darkness to light. When this happens, God has come to you and you can live in this revived state until Messiah comes for His glorious church. As a matter fact, my wife, Barbara just told me that revival is a lifestyle – it's walking in the light of the glorious gospel of Jesus Christ daily.

THE LIGHT HAS COME

"Arise, shine for *thy light is come*, and the glory of the Lord is risen upon thee" (Isaiah 60:1).

While Yochanan was baptizing the multitude of new converts, Yeshua decides to come to where he was. He tells Yochanan to baptize Him too. I have a question for all of my pastor friends. Can you imagine being the person to baptize Jesus? Yochanan didn't feel like "I'm the man now." He didn't

---

[8] Pp. 162-163, Intercessory Prayer, Pastor Dutch Sheets, Regal Books, 1957 Eastman Avenue, Ventura, California 93003, copyright 1197.

put on his personal website, "I baptized the Messiah." He didn't demand the presbyter to elevate him to the office of an apostle since he did something great. As righteous a man that Yochanan was, He didn't feel entitled, but unworthy to even untie the Messiah's shoelaces.

After His baptism, the Holy Spirit leads Yeshua into the wilderness of Judaea. He spent 40 days there in fasting and prayer. After enduring the temptations of Lucifer himself, angels came and ministered unto Him (Matthew 4:11) and He comes out of the wilderness in the power of the Holy Spirit (Luke 4:14) into Galilee and expands the revival that Yochanan started along the Jordan River. He picks up the revival after hearing of Yochanan being imprisoned. Many of the people who followed Yochanan began to follow Yeshua because he told them that Yeshua was mightier than he (Matthew 3:11). He exhorted his disciples that he must decrease and Yeshua must increase (John 3:30). The fame (news) of Yeshua spread throughout all the region of Galilee (Luke 4:14) and Syria (Matthew 4:24). Yeshua is now preaching revival in this region. He was:

1. Teaching in the synagogues and preaching the good news of the kingdom,
2. Healing all sicknesses and diseases, and
3. Delivering those possessed by demons.

Before you know it, a great multitude was following Him. They came from everywhere; from Galilee, Decapolis, Jerusalem, Judaea and beyond the Jordan. Here is a church growth strategy

Chapter Five - Let in the Light

that you may not learn in conferences today – teach and preach kingdom, heal the sick and deliver those possessed by demons. J. I. Packer says, "Revival is the near presence of God giving new power to the gospel of sin and grace."[9] Yeshua expanded the revival of Yochanan the Baptizer by the working of miracles and healing. They both preached repentance, but Yeshua had the power of the Holy Spirit with Him to work miracles.

Matthew attributes this prophecy of Esaias (Isaiah) to Yeshua of Nazareth: "And leaving Nazareth, he came and dwelt in Capernaum, which is upon the sea coast, in the borders of Zabulon and Nephthalim: that it might be fulfilled which was spoken by Esaias the prophet, saying, the land of Zabulon, and the land of Nephthalim, by the way of the sea, beyond Jordan, Galilee of the Gentiles; the people which sat in darkness saw *great light;* and to them which sat in the region and shadow of death *light is sprung up"* (Matthew 4:13-16).

Matthew identified Yeshua of Nazareth as the light that Isaiah was prophesying about. He is the light that must be received for a changed heart. He is the light that we should let into our hearts.

The light, Yeshua, sprung up in Israel in a time unexpected by them. God surprised them. The very moment when God will come where you are is undetermined by you. Prophets will prophesy of His coming, prayer warriors will pray for His coming and pastors will try to posture the church for His

---

[9] J.I. Packer, "The Glory of God and the Reviving of Religion" in A God-Entranced Vision of All Things (pp. 100-104)

coming, but no one knows the exact time when He will actually show up. Oh, but when He does (and He will), get ready for miracles, signs and wonders, healings, salvation and deliverance from the bondage of sin.

If the world around you is dark; if the influence of sin and evil has intensified, then you are a candidate for light to come to where you are. Check your heart, your home, your community, your church, your city and your nation and see how dark it is. That darkness is an indicator that light is needed and it's an opportunity for light to come. You may be the one that the Lord is awakening to prayer and repentance to usher in the greatest revival in your region.

The apostle Yochanan (not the Baptizer) says, "In Him (Yeshua) was life; and the life was the light of men" (John 1:4). True and genuine life is embodied in Messiah. Without His life in us we "sit in darkness… in the region and shadow of death." Yeshua also made claim to being The Light. He says, "I am The Light of the world: he that followeth Me shall not walk in darkness, but shall have the light of life" (John 8:12).

THE BIG QUESTION

Now, I must ask you some questions that are pivotal for reading the remainder of this book. Are you still walking in darkness? Are you living in sin? Do you have an intimate relationship with Yeshua the Messiah (Jesus Christ)? Have you let the light shine into your heart? Have the eyes of your understanding been enlightened? Are you experiencing a personal revival yet? As you take a personal assessment of where you are today, do you have a lukewarm faith or are you on fire for God? Does your faith seem alive or dead? How often do you pray and study the word of God? How excited are you to attend church to fellowship with God's people? When was the last time you fasted? How often do you share the good news of Yeshua?

The reason why I am asking these questions is because you are the person that God has chosen to help usher in regional revival. Your home, church and city need you. You are significant in changing the atmosphere of your region. Spiritual awakening starts with you. Revival is a lifestyle and you can turn your life around right now and posture your entire being toward the living God from this day forward. It's time to renew your faith in Yeshua and return to your first love. This is not just a book but a prophetic message to those who the Father desires to use for the next move of God. Remember, *revival is God touching minds and hearts in an arresting, devastating, exalting way, to draw them to Himself through working from the inside out rather than from the outside in.* Arise, shine, for thy light is come!

Chapter Six

How to Know if God is Calling You to Revival

Many people have the misunderstanding that the beginning of revival is when miracles suddenly break out in their churches or meeting places. This is far from the truth. Miracles are a byproduct of revival not the beginning of it. Because of this misconception, many intercessors and believers get discouraged when they don't see immediate results of miracles, healings, signs and wonders. So, as a warning, do not look for miracles to happen right away. That is a grave error.

As I said before, repentance is the forerunner for revival. You can know that God is calling you to revival when He burdens your heart to repent before Him. Revival cannot be manufactured. It is more than a feel-good service. It is a lifestyle. Once a group of people begin to walk in this lifestyle, the atmosphere around them will shift and make way for the presence of God.

This burden to repent comes from the Holy Spirit. It's the drawing power of the Father. The Father makes a decision to draw you by making you sensitive and aware of the need for more of Him. Yeshua says, "No man can come to Me, except the Father which hath sent Me *draw* him" (John 6:44). You will know when God is calling you to revival when:

1. He awakens you to the reality of your present sinful condition and causes you to experience brokenness.
2. He awakens you to the reality of the kingdom of God and your desperate need of Him and causes you to have great expectation of His coming.

BROKENNESS

This burden of the Holy Spirit will stay with you until you come to a place of pure spiritual brokenness. Spiritual brokenness is to be crushed or hurt in your spirit over your sins. It is to be aware of and feel awful about grieving the heart of your loving Father. "For thus says the high and exalted One Who lives forever, whose name is Holy, "I dwell on a high and holy place, and also with the contrite and lowly of spirit in order *to revive the spirit of the lowly and to revive the heart of the contrite."* - (Isaiah 57:15 NASB)

A DISOBEDIENT SON

I remember when I did a terrible thing as a teen that really disappointed my father. My parents had gone out of town and I decided to go against their instructions of not having any guest in the house while they were away. You can probably already sense that I did something terribly stupid. Well, you're right. A sense of freedom to do whatever I wanted to do came upon me. Lo and behold, I decided to invite two of my friends over to the house.

Now, you need to know that I didn't grow up in a devoutly Christian home. We were the sporadic attendees of a Baptist Church that we claimed membership to. Yep, we were CME Christians – the ones who attend church only on Christmas, Mother's Day and Easter. We were the average African-American household, scratching and surviving, like the Evans family of the TV sitcom, Good Times. We were just lucky we got 'em – good times that is. And on this particular day, I had a J. J. Evans knuckleheaded moment.

Everything seemed fine; my friends and I were on our best behavior. We just watched television and cracked jokes and did what the average teenage friends would do – just hanging out with each other. Until … well, someone got thirsty. And it just so happen that my father had a bar loaded with alcoholic beverages. We wanted more than just Kool-Aid this time. So we took it upon ourselves to go to the bar and get a sip of something stronger than the cherry-flavored, sugar drink in the fridge. One sip of that *Knottyhead* Gin led to a couple of glasses full. The sad thing about it is that we didn't even know we were drunk.

One of my friends suggested that we should go see our girlfriends. They lived about 5-10 miles away. You should know, we weren't in the mood to walk and neither one of us had a vehicle to drive. How did we get to there? We decided to ride bicycles. Well, we didn't get far out of our neighborhood before one of my friends tumbled over his bicycle and smacked his face against the hard tar-paved street. He busted his lip open and bled feverishly. Somehow my other friend and I managed to get him to his house. His sister (who was his guardian) interrogated us but we held faithfully to our fib that we were playing football in the street and he tripped up and fell. I don't know why we were convinced she'd bought our story as slamming the door in our face while cussing up a storm.

A DISAPPOINTED FATHER

My parents returned back home and received a phone call. I'm sure they heard the same curse words from the caller who was, of course, my friend's sister. She threatened to sue my parents because her brother was a minor who got drunk in our home. My father, who was not saved at the time, seemed as though he found some new curse words as he shouted them in my direction. And although he punished me, I can see the look of anger his face turn to disappointment.

That disappointing look followed by what seemed to be the silent treatment is what hurt the most. I think every time I glanced at him, his demeanor did not seem to waver. This went on for a good while (it could've only been a day or two but seemed like forever) until he decided to break the code of silence and speak to me again. All the while, I was embarrassed and felt so bad to see my father look the way he did in disgust toward me, especially when I knew that I was the cause of his pain.

My friend, this is called brokenness. It is when you are crushed in your spirit after realizing the pain you have caused someone else. When we realize that we have hurt the heart of our heavenly Father by our disobedience and embarrassing acts it should break our hearts. Until you come to a place of brokenness, God cannot use you for revival.

Today, believers are not crushed by the effects of their awful sins that hurt the heart of God. You can tell when the Lord desires to revive you and to use you for citywide revival because the Holy Spirit will heavily convict you of the sins that brought our heavenly Father pain. You will not only be convicted of your sins but experience a level of pain from realizing how disappointed the Father really is.

A HURTING FATHER

My son, Randy, recalls the time when he had to break some "not-so-godly" news to me and my wife. At the time, he was traveling with a well-known artist. He met a nice, beautiful young Christian girl (who eventually became his wife). They fell in love. But being young, on the road, and without strong accountability, he and his newly found girlfriend had a pleasurable moment and the result was pregnancy out of wedlock.

Sitting in our living room, he finally shared the "not-so-godly" news with me; I was angry and went into strongly reproving them. After my long lecture of what they already knew, I could feel myself being disappointed. Randy was also looking like a lost puppy saddened by the disappointment he could see on my face and to know he was the cause of my downward disposition.

I can remember that pain of disappointment. I remember feeling disregarded for everything that I taught him. I remember the sorrow of knowing the consequences he may face. I remember the distance it put between us in that moment and the feeling of not knowing what else to say.

But here is a key revelation: I can remember seeing how Randy went from initially being guarded, to bracing for the lecture, to sadness, to not knowing what to say to me and then to a place of brokenness and wishing to hear my voice reassuring him that I hadn't given up on him. He wanted to know that we can still have those close conversations and that my love for him had not diminished because of his moral collapse. He needed me desperately, and as a father, I could sense it. He was broken. I could hear it in his voice and see it upon his countenance. He did not know what to do.

Chapter Six - How to Know if God is Calling You to Revival

Have you ever felt so distant from our heavenly Father that you just didn't know what to pray for, or better yet, that your penitent prayer did not appear to be reaching His ear? Has He ever kept silent during a time you felt you needed to hear his voice the most? Were you hurt when you realized your compromise and disregard to the things which He had taught you is what made Him avoid acknowledging you? That broken fellowship ultimately caused you to have a broken heart.

Here's the good news – just like I could sense my son's brokenness, our heavenly Father can sense ours. As a matter of fact, that's what made me initiate a fresh heartfelt conversation with him. The Lord is looking for broken hearts to mend (Luke 4:18). He is looking for people who need Him desperately. Are you at a point where you need Him desperately? His distance and silence has created a thirst in you.

Revival begins not only with being aware of how you've hurt the heart of God but of having a deep longing for being reconciled with Him. If you are in this condition you are a candidate for revival.

YOU DID IT, SO OWN IT!

I love to use King David as a prime example of spiritual brokenness. The Lord had evaluated King David's heart. Although outwardly to everyone else he seemed okay, but inwardly he was in a deep struggle of sorrow for the sins he committed. Yes, the man who was after God's own heart was in a backslidden condition. No one knows the reason why he concealed his sins. Perhaps, it was his national status and position as king of Israel that he felt the need to keep his sins unnoticed by any man. David had plotted a wicked scheme to have his captain, Uriah the Hittite, go off into battle on the frontline while intentionally having sexual relations with the man's wife, Bathsheba.

The Lord had enough of seeing his anointed in a backslidden state. So, he sends a prophet to confront David with the purpose of bringing him to a place of repentance. Nathan cleverly reproves David. He begins to narrate to him an incident that took place between two men in one city; one rich, the other poor. The rich man had abundant livestock but the poor man had only one little female lamb that he bought and nourished up. This little lamb grew up with him and his children like a favorite pet, eating and drinking with family and lying in his master's lap. She was just like a daughter to the poor man.

One day, the rich man was having a traveler come to visit him for dinner. Instead of taking a lamb from his own flock, the rich man decided to take the poor man's lamb to slaughter it and prepare it for their supper.

While the prophet was speaking, King David was boiling in anger against the rich man. He was so much into the story that he spoke up and said, "As the Lord liveth, the man that hath done this thing shall surely die: and he shall restore the lamb fourfold because he did this thing, and because he had no pity" (2 Samuel 12:5-6).

Chapter Six - How to Know if God is Calling You to Revival

David, not knowing that this was a complete setup, fell right into the prophetic trap. The prophet reproves him, "Thou art the man!" Then he drills right into David's heart the revelation of the depths of his sin. He speaks on God's behalf telling him how great of favor the Lord poured upon him. He told him how the Lord anointed him to be king, how he delivered him from Saul, how he gave him his master's house and wives and how he gave him both the house of Israel and Judah. And if that wasn't enough for him the Lord would give him whatever else he desired. Can you see how disgusted David was feeling about himself? He knew the Lord was hurt just by reminding him of how good he's been to him especially when he was just a little, rejected lad cleaning sheep dung for his father, Jesse.

But if that wasn't enough, the Lord goes on to tell David that he *despised* his commandment (v.9) and Himself (v. 10). This really showed David how disappointed the Lord was about his actions. He said that David despised Him and His word. This word "despise" in Hebrew is *bazah* which means *"to make of little account; to treat contemptuously or scornfully."* It's like an attorney in a courtroom who disregards the instructions of a judge and continues to say or do something contrary to what the judge had ruled. That attorney despised the judge and his word. The judge usually shouts out a warning that he will hold him in contempt. To be contemptuous, the attorney would ignore the judge and continue on past the warning. How many of us are like the bad attorney and ignore the warnings of the Lord to stop our sinful actions? You, like David, are in contempt, despising the Lord and His word.

The good news is that the Lord had enough of David's foolishness and cover up. It was the Lord, out of His deep love for David, who decided that he was going to make things right. If it wasn't for the Lord's decision to send a prophet to David for reconciliation, things could have escalated to a whole other level of darkness and chaos. It was the decision of a loving Father to forgive David and revive him. This led David to a place of brokenness. He began to own up to his sin and confess them before the Lord. He cried to the prophet Nathan, "I have sinned against the Lord" (v. 13). David realized how his sins affected the heart of a Father who treated him so favorably, who didn't deserve being mistreated and devalued.

THE PURPOSE OF BROKENNESS

We read in Psalm 51 where King David is really longing for renewal in his relationship with God. His awful sins caused a disconnect in His fellowship with God. He couldn't praise God like he used to. The excitement wasn't there. His joy had dissipated. He pens his lament in this Psalm:

> "Have mercy upon me, O God, according to thy lovingkindness: according unto the multitude of thy tender mercies blot out my transgressions. Wash me thoroughly from mine iniquity, and cleanse me from my sin. For I acknowledge my transgressions: and my sin is ever before me. Against thee, thee only, have

Chapter Six - How to Know if God is Calling You to Revival

I sinned, and done this evil in thy sight: that thou mightiest be justified when thou speakest, and be clear when thou judgest. Behold, I was shapen in iniquity; and in sin did my mother conceive me. Behold, thou desirest truth in the inward parts: and in the hidden part thou shalt make me to know wisdom. Purge me with hyssop, and I shall be clean: wash me, and I shall be whiter than snow. Make me to hear joy and gladness; that the bones which thou hast broken may rejoice. Hide thy face from my sins, and blot out all mine iniquities. Create in me a clean heart, O God; and renew a right spirit within me. Cast me not away from thy presence; and take not thy holy spirit from me. Restore unto me the joy of thy salvation; and uphold me with thy free spirit." (Psalm 51:1-12)

This Psalm shows how much David yearned for that intimacy with God that he forfeited by his own wickedness. It is this condition of abasement and contrition that moves the heart of God. "The sacrifices of God are of a broken heart. A broken and a contrite spirit, O God, You will not despise" (Psalm 51:17 NASB). God will not turn away a heart that's broken for Him. It becomes a sacrifice that He is willing to accept. He draws near and revives the brokenhearted (Psalm 34:18; Isaiah 57:15).

The purpose of spiritual brokenness is to get you to see how desperately you need Abba. It is to get you to turn toward Him and reestablish a growing, intimate relationship with Him. It creates a deep level of genuine repentance and then a hunger and passionate desire for His nearness. He helps remove your spiritual apathy and lukewarmness. At the same time, the Father's heart moves from disappointment in you to delight in you. You become a sacrifice that He cannot refuse (Psalm 51:17). Your brokenness is your signal to the Father that you are ready to draw near to Him. In return, He is ready to draw near to you. If you're broken, He promises to be near. He will come to where you are.

Chapter Seven

His Name is Jealous

"You shall worship no other god, for the Lord whose name is Jealous is a jealous God."
(Exodus 34:14)

There are many attributes that we can ascribe to the character of God. We comfortably worship Him for His splendor and the uniqueness of His omnipotence, omniscience, omnipresence and the splendor of His glory. He's majestic and sovereign. We know Him to be holy, righteous and perfect in all His ways. He's good and full of compassion. He's merciful and gracious.

He's a loving God. He's faithful and just; patient and longsuffering. I can go on and on about the awesome character of God. However, there is one attribute that we rarely want to notice about God as though it makes Him seem less God or something. It kind of seems negative and disrespectful to call God *jealous*.

The fact that God is a jealous God should not be taken negatively. You may be wondering, "Isn't jealousy a bad trait? Doesn't it have an undertone of selfishness and distrust?" We've been programmed to think of jealousy only in a negative way. When we think of jealousy, we immediately think of an enraged spouse who distrusts their spouse for talking to anyone. That's actually control and possessiveness, associated with that distrust. This often leads to marital abuse and manipulation. Our psyche cannot fathom God being this way. This cannot be the reason why God is a jealous God. God is not controlling, possessive or distrusting.

There are two aspects of the word jealousy. There is the *sin of jealousy* and there is *justified jealousy* which is *passion exerted from the violation of an exclusive devotion (relationship)*. I will explain the difference between the two.

THE SIN OF JEALOUSY

The sin of jealousy is when you desire something that someone else possesses. It can also be a hatred of the person because you feel they don't deserve what they have but you deserve it instead. The word envious (envy) is used interchangeably with jealousy.

Chapter Seven - His Name is Jealous

The Philistines were jealous of Isaac because he had flocks, herds and servants (Genesis 26:14). Rachel was jealous of Leah because she was producing children for Jacob while she was barren (Genesis 30:1). Joseph's brothers were jealous (envious) of him because his father favored him over them and because he dreamed of having authority over them (Genesis 37:1-11). In these cases, we see the sin of jealousy. The Philistines, Rachel, and Joseph's brothers all desired something that someone else had and hated them for it.

Our God is not this way. He doesn't desire what anyone else has. He doesn't hate you or think He deserves something that someone else possesses. Who would serve a god who gets jealous by that definition? It would be rather ridiculous. So what does the Bible mean by God being jealous and why is it important in the context of revival?

JUSTIFIED JEALOUSY

The other type of jealousy is what I call *justified jealousy*. This kind of jealousy is only found where there is a covenant of exclusivity. In fact, it doesn't stem from hate, but love. We usually see this passionate aspect of love when the covenant of exclusivity is violated.

In the Bible, the word jealous is *qannâ'* in Hebrew (OT) and *zelos* in Greek (NT). It carries the idea of *a burning heat*. This is why Moses declared, "Our God is *a consuming fire* (Deuteronomy 4:24). Burning heat signifies passion. Unfortunately, it's a passion released when love has been trampled upon. It comes in the form of anger. The doctrinal belief that God never gets angry is false. No one wants to be cheated on, trampled over, taken advantage of or violated – not even God. The Lord's anger is kindled when we are unfaithful to Him. He has every right to be jealous when we reject His love for another.

For God, jealousy is His passionate love that cannot bear any other love within the heart of His people. He's the Lover of our soul and His love demands an exclusive devotion. If we're going to be carriers of revival then we must realize the jealousy of God.

JEALOUSY PROVOKED

Jealousy has to be provoked. God's anger has to be stirred up. He doesn't just get angry at any little thing. He's patient, kind and longsuffering. He's full of joy. Being angry is the last thing on His mind. He wants to give us the world. We are the apple of His eye. There is but one thing that frustrates the love of God and that one thing is idolatry.

Yahweh made a covenant with Israel and it was a covenant of exclusivity. In other words, you could not give devotion or worship to any other god. This covenant is found in Exodus 20:1-6:

> Then God spoke all these words, saying, "I am the Lord your God, who brought you out of the land of Egypt, out of the house of slavery. *You shall have no*

other gods before Me. You shall not make for yourself an idol, or any likeness of what is in heaven above or on the earth beneath or in the water under the earth. You shall not worship them or serve them; *for I, the Lord your God, am a jealous God,* visiting the iniquity of the fathers on the children, on the third and the fourth generations of those who hate Me, but showing lovingkindness to thousands, to those who love Me and keep My commandments" (NASB, italics added).

He reiterates the covenant of exclusivity in Exodus 34:14:

"You shall worship no other god, for the Lord *whose name is Jealous* is *a jealous God."*

We agreed to the terms of the covenant. It's like a marriage and idolatry is spiritual infidelity. God's attribute of jealousy only comes out when we worship, serve or give our devotion to another god, person or thing. His jealousy has to be stirred (provoked). In Deuteronomy 32:16 (NASB), Moses declares, *"They made Him jealous* with strange gods; with abominations they provoked Him to anger." In verse 21, God confirms Moses' claim, *"They have made Me jealous* with what is not God; they have provoked Me to anger with their idols."

Idolatry is breaking our covenant agreement with God and stirs up His anger. Because He's a merciful God, He sends prophets to tell us about our wayward condition. If we don't listen to the prophet and continue in our idolatry, then He brings a warning of pending judgment. If we persist in our idolatry and devotion to another and fail to heed the warning, then He chastens us. Finally, if we reject the prophets, the warnings and chastening, judgment comes.

THE SPIRIT YEARNS

A sincere repentance, heartfelt love for, and commitment to be exclusively devoted to Him is what He searches for. Revival is returning to our first love (Revelation 2:4-5). The Lord searches for people who are willing to be exclusively devoted to Him.

"For the eyes of the Lord run to and fro throughout the whole earth, to show himself strong in the behalf of them whose heart is perfect toward him" (2 Chronicles 16:9). I actually like how the New American Standard Bible translates this verse. It says that the Lord is searching the earth *"to strongly support those whose heart is completely His."*

This is the Lord's desire – to strongly support His people. All He wants is for us to give Him our complete devotion, to be completely His. This is what I believe the Apostle James was referring to when he asks, "Do you think that the Scripture says in vain, 'The Spirit who dwells in us yearns jealously?'" (James 4:5, NKJV). I can see the love of God written all over this verse. The Lord yearns for our exclusive devotion. He strongly supports those who give them their utmost devotion. James immediately says afterward, "But He gives more grace…God resists the proud, but gives grace unto the humble" (James 4:6). Grace is the Lord favoring us and doing something for us that we cannot do in our own strength or human capacity. It sounds like James was saying the same thing the author of Second Chronicles was saying, "He strongly supports those whose heart is completely His." Will you give Him your wholehearted devotion? Will you return to your first love? When you do revival will begin in you. When you do, God will come to where you are.

Chapter Eight

Draw Near to God

This section of the book will deal primarily with what we should do once we sense the burden of revival has come upon us. You will see how your life should take shape in order to encounter His closeness and to experience the working of His mighty power personally, and to help extend it abroad. Revival starts with you.

DEEP CALLS UNTO DEEP

> *"Deep calls to deep at the sound of Your waterfalls; all Your breakers and Your waves have rolled over me."*
> (Psalm 42:7 NASB)

David was apparently in a low moment in his life because he writes of his soul being "cast down" and "disquieted" in him (Psalm 42:5, 6). The way I picture verse 7 is David sensing God's love cascading upon the depths of his weary heart like the heavy waters flushing down a waterfall. The reality of His lovingkindness rolls over him like a castaway being hit by a tidal wave along the seashore. David was awakening to the reality of God's love that washed away the weariness of his soul and feeling so distant from God. His thirsty soul was being filled. This is what happens when Yeshua quickens us to revival. He jolts us from our sleep, snapping us out of our mundane, apathetic and casual Christianity.

J. I. Packer makes this powerful statement about revival:

> *"It is the Holy Spirit sensitizing souls to divine realities and so generating deep-level responses to God in the form of faith and repentance, praise and prayer, love and joy,*

Chapter Eight - Draw Near to God

works of benevolence and service and initiatives of outreach and sharing."[10]

Here, in J. I. Packer's statement about revival there are two essential things that take place:

1. <u>The Holy Spirit sensitizes our souls to divine realities</u>. Revival is when God awakens the spiritually insensitive soul that was lured to sleep by enjoying the pleasures of this world or distracted by the cares of life. The heart and mind is awakened by the Spirit of God to realities that are in God's heart, what's on His mind for this season. These divine realities are what God desires, His intended purposes, what He plans to do. The Apostle Paul calls them "the things of the Spirit" (Romans 8:5) and "the deep things of God" (1 Corinthians 2:9-10).

2. <u>A deep-level response to God is generated</u>. The heart that is awakened has an earnest response that becomes evident through acts of genuine repentance, intense praise, and fervent prayers, along with showing love, outreach initiatives and sharing the good news and giving more generously to support the work of the kingdom and the furtherance of the gospel.

---

[10] J.I. Packer, "The Glory of God and the Reviving of Religion" in A God-Entranced Vision of All Things (pp. 100-104)

DRAWING NEAR TO GOD

The above is an example of a heart that has "drawn near" to God. "Draw near to God, and He will draw near to you" (James 4:8 NKJV). God promises that He will "draw near" to those who draw near to Him (James 4:8). The key is getting God to come where you are. Thus, He cannot deny His word of drawing near to us when He sees us making intentional efforts to draw near to Him. After all, it is through His initial act of "sensitizing" our sleeping spirit to His realities that we have the opportunity to respond to Him. How are you responding to Him? When He sees our heart responding in a "drawing near" way, you can anticipate Him to come your way.

The Apostle James shares with us *how* we can draw near to God. He shows a heart responding to the call of God to revival:

> *"Cleanse your hands, ye sinners; and purify your hearts, ye double minded. Be afflicted, and mourn, and weep: let your laughter be turned to mourning, and your joy to heaviness. Humble yourselves in the sight of the Lord, and He shall lift you up."*
> (James 4:8-10)

There are four things he mentions here as something we can do intentionally to show God that we are drawing near to Him and will cause God's response of coming to where we are:

Chapter Eight - Draw Near to God

1. Cleanse your hands
2. Purify your hearts
3. Be afflicted, mourn and weep
4. Humble yourselves

First, let me say that James was writing this to believers. He calls the believers "sinners" and "double minded." That may not work in our churches today. James may never get invited back to some prominent pulpits across America. We are too afraid to call a spade a spade. We are threatened by the fact that they may leave our pews and take their tithes with them. The reality is we need more preachers like James. Revival comes when we call a spade a spade, when we "cry aloud and spare not."

CLEANSE YOURSELF

James was calling for a response to knowing that the Spirit yearns jealously for our exclusive devotion. Sinners (Greek *hamartolo)*, he proclaims, are those who are *devoted to sin, habitual sinners, or morally wicked.* It is someone who simply enjoys the pleasures of living carnally and has made true fellowship with God of little importance. We expect this naturally from someone who doesn't know God or has not been born again, but not from a believer. We should desire intimacy with God and growth in our character and walk with Him. We would be fooling ourselves if we desire and are indulged in fornication, adultery, pornography, witchcraft, calling psychic hotlines for readings, idolatry, getting drunk, and being greedy for material gain, etc. while thinking that we are going to fellowship with God. The Apostle John penned, "If we say that we have fellowship with Him, and walk in darkness, we lie, and do not the truth" (1 John 1:6). We cannot be *devoted* to sin and devoted to God at the same time if we want Him to draw near to us. This hinders revival.

James tells us to *"cleanse our hands."* The hands being cleansed are hands free from external acts of sin. The hands signify works, deeds, conduct, lifestyle, etc. There has to be deliberate and sincere efforts to clean up our lives.

The word used for "cleanse" is *katharizo* which means to *"free yourself from every corruption or corrupt desires."* Descriptively, it is like a vine cleansed by pruning and thus made fit to bear fruit." As long as we are enjoying and indulged in the pleasures of sin, we will not be fit to live a fruitful life in Christ. We will be bearing the wrong kind of fruit and sending the wrong signal to others that God doesn't mind us living the kind of lifestyle we want to and expect Him to do great things for us. Let us examine ourselves to see what we can rid from our lives that is displeasing to God. When we do this, when we take the cleansing power of His word and apply it to our lives, He promises to draw near to us.

PURIFY YOUR HEART

In addition to James telling the sinner to cleanse his hands, he tells the *doubleminded* to purify their hearts. The word used here for doubleminded is *"dipsuchos"* which translates as "having two

Chapter Eight - Draw Near to God

souls." It's not that you're schizophrenic, but simply that you have a divided interest. It's not so much of having intellectual doubt as it is doubt about commitment. James was calling out the believer who demonstrates a wavering commitment – sometimes wanting to go all out for God and sometimes, well, you can't find them nowhere near God or His church. They become too invested and preoccupied with other things that captivate their interest above their commitment to God.

This cannot be the case when you've been awakened to divine realities. The Lord awakens us and tells us to make up our minds. You can't depend on a doubleminded person. James says that a doubleminded person is unstable in all his ways (James 1:8). He's too fickle and indecisive. You ask them to do something and they initially say yes. Before you know it, you get a phone call and they have changed their mind. Ask yourself, "Can God depend on me? Can He trust me with revival?" Yeshua taught on the impossibility of serving two masters (Matthew 6:24, Luke 16:13). He also taught that we have to be single-hearted toward God (Matthew 6:22, Luke 11:34). King David and Apostle Paul both expressed their singlehearted devotion toward God. They had a "one thing" attitude (Psalm 27:4; Philippians 3:13). Singlehearted devotion will eliminate doublemindedness.

In order for me to get to a place where I'm no longer doubleminded, and my commitment to God has been settled, James says I have to *"purify my heart."* The heart has to be consecrated to God as sacred. We draw near to God by sanctifying our hearts and setting it apart for His desires and His pleasures.

The Apostle John lets us in on a secret on how to purify our hearts. He says, "He that hath this hope in Him will purify himself even as He is pure" (1 John 3:3). The secret to purifying the heart is "hope in Him." The Greek word for "hope" is *elpizo* which means "cheerful anticipation or confident expectation." Now that Yeshua has awakened you to divine realities and has promised you that He will draw near to you and let you experience revival, personally and in your church and region, you can take these promises and begin to look within your heart, see what's keeping you from being fully committed to Him and utterly destroy it. Consecrate and dedicate your heart for one thing – exclusive devotion to God.

BE AFFLICTED, MOURN AND WEEP

A wholehearted drawing near to God can be found through "afflicting yourself, mourning and weeping." In the Old Testament, the prophet Joel heralded similar words to an unrepentant Israel in lieu of the "day of the Lord" which was believed to be Yahweh coming to execute judgment. Joel prophesies:

"And the Lord shall utter His voice before His army: for His camp is very great: for He is strong that executeth His word: for the day of the Lord is great and very terrible; and who can abide it? Therefore also now, saith the Lord, turn ye even to me with *all your heart*, and with *fasting*, and with *weeping*, and with

Chapter Eight - Draw Near to God

mourning: and *rend your heart,* and not your garments, and turn unto the Lord your God: for he is gracious and merciful, slow to anger, and of great kindness, and repenteth Him of the evil. Who knoweth if He will return and repent, and leave a blessing behind Him" (Joel 2:11-14, italics added).

Joel was calling for the nation to repent and turn to God with fasting, weeping and mourning. This is the act of *rending* the heart; it's expressing how torn your heart is over the sins that kept you distant from fellowship with God. What makes it worse is that we were enjoying it. James said we had "laughter and joy." We may have such a good time in the pleasurable things of this life that we fail to see how far removed we were from divine realities. We must rend our hearts before Yeshua rends the heavens and come down.

James admonishes us to *"afflict ourselves."* This is synonymous with *"fasting."* We should turn to God with fasting. Giving up food for a certain length of time shows God how desperate you want Him. It shows Him that you are serious about being in intimate fellowship with Him. Fasting gets us closer to God. Moses fasted. David fasted. Daniel fasted. Yeshua fasted. The apostles also fasted. The New Testament church fasted. Fasting helps us discipline ourselves with self-denial. It teaches us to make our bodies subject to what God sees as important.

James says we should also *mourn* and *weep.* There has to be some kind of remorse and godly sorrow concerning the pleasures of sin that lured us away from our exclusive devotion to God. We must ask the Holy Spirit to help us see these sinful pleasures as awful and to help us look upon them in disgust. How can we enjoy them any longer when they, in fact, have blinded us from having a pure, authentic and unhindered fellowship with our Father?

The good news is that we can anticipate encountering Yeshua again. Joel said that if we fast, mourn and weep, our gracious, merciful, patient and kind God may turn aside and stop the calamity (evil) assigned to our disobedience and instead leave a blessing behind (Joel 2:13-14)!

HUMBLE YOURSELF

The final way that we can openly demonstrate our drawing near to God is through *humbling ourselves*. Webster's Dictionary defines humble (humility) as being made lower in condition or status. It also carries the idea of "destroying strength" so that you would develop the need to depend upon another. We have areas of pride in our lives that makes us rely upon our own strength in accomplishing things outside of God's assistance. We often use wealth, fame, popularity, family status, education, titles and positions of authority to keep us propped up and looking strong. These are just some of the pride props that the Lord has to knock down in order to get us to solely trust and depend upon Him.

Pride is living independent from the life of God. Simply put, we just don't need Him. Revival begins when we deal with our own pride and realize our dire need for God. The Apostle James alerts us that God resists the proud (James 4:6). If we

Chapter Eight - Draw Near to God

don't take the initiative to examine our lives and deal with our own pride issues, then the Lord will be happy to assist us. I must warn you – His method of humbling us is far more challenging than if we just take the initiative to deal with it ourselves.

James says although God resists the proud, He gives grace to the humble (James 4:6). Grace is God's undeserving favor based primarily upon the fact that He sent His Son, Yeshua, to redeem us from the hand of the enemy and the bondage of sin and has reconciled us unto Himself that we may have eternal life. "When we were yet *without strength*, in due time Christ died for the ungodly" (Romans 5:8).

Secondarily, grace is the supernatural power to do something that you could not do in your own strength. It is God's divine intervention and His supernatural power working on our behalf. He helps the humble. When we have no conceivable way of accomplishing certain things on our own, the Lord comes to our aid and does it for us. This is the heart of Revival. We can't save our loved ones, we can't heal those with terminal cancer or a dreadful disease, and we can't change certain circumstances, grow our churches or change our city. There are just certain things that are out of our control and beyond our capability. We must rely on God to do it. Revival is ignited when people humble themselves and cry out to God for Him to come and do what we cannot do in our own strength.

Moses reveals the secret to why Yahweh led them through the wilderness. It was to humble them, examine them, reveal what was in their hearts and let them realize that man cannot live by bread alone, but by every word that proceeds out of His mouth (Deuteronomy 8:2, 3). The wilderness was all about their humility and getting them to trust in the Lord and His word. The Lord had them undergo life-threatening situations – the dry, scorching heat, limited access to food and water, threats of wild beasts, poisonous snakes and scorpions, and no weapons to fight against lurking enemies.

If they were going to make it out of the wilderness and into the land flowing with milk and honey, they had to humble themselves, realize that they didn't have the capacity to change anything and that they had to solely rely on God and His word. The same goes for you and me. If you want to experience Revival, you must humble yourself, confront your pride and begin to rely solely upon the Lord, His word and His power.

Chapter Nine

Diligently Seek Him

"Without faith, it is impossible to please Him: for he that cometh to God must believe that He is, and that He is a rewarder of them that diligently seek Him."
(Hebrews 11:6)

PLEASING GOD

From the above Scripture we can safely say that faith involves *pleasing* God. The author of Hebrews says, "Without *faith* it is impossible to *please* Him. He left us an endearing example of a man who had God-pleasing faith. Then he gives clues to what this God-pleasing faith looks like. Isn't it amazing to know that YOU can please God! Yes, *you* can please the same God that created the heavens and the earth, parted the Red Sea, stopped the mouth of lions, fed 5,000 people with two fish and five loaves of bread, healed the sick, caused the blind to see, the deaf to hear, and raised Lazarus from the dead! Do not sell yourself short. Remove the impossibility of pleasing God away from your mind. The Lord did not save you just to turn around and be displeased with you. Make it your goal to please Him every day. There are two promises I found in the word of God as it relates to pleasing Him:

1. <u>We will receive whatever we request Him to do for us</u>. "And whatsoever we ask, we receive of him, because we keep his commandments, and do those things that are pleasing in his sight" (1 John 3:22).
2. <u>You will live a peaceful life</u>. "When a man's ways please the Lord, he maketh even his enemies to be at peace with him" (Proverbs 16:7).

THE MAN WHO PLEASED GOD

Living a life of exclusive devotion to God pleases Him. This is what Enoch did. He is our endearing example of someone pleasing God. His wholehearted devotion left an indelible mark

Chapter Nine - Diligently Seek Him

on the heart of God. "... for before his translation he [Enoch] had this testimony, that he pleased God" (Hebrews 11:5).

I searched the book of Genesis which recorded the story of Enoch to see what he did to please God and all it says is that he *"walked with God"* (Genesis 5:22, 24). The secret is found in the Hebrew verb *"hâlak"* which is translated "walked" and it denotes *intimate fellowship with God*. So it could very well read, "And Enoch lived in intimate fellowship with God." This is the key to pleasing God. To draw near to God requires us to look at our "walk," our fellowship with Him. Are we fellowshipping with Him on a daily basis?

Jerry Bridges, when explaining godliness, calls Enoch's example of walking with God, "devotion in action." He goes on to say that godliness conveys the idea of a personal attitude toward God that *results in actions that are pleasing to God.*[11] He also quotes, "His [Enoch's] walk with God speaks of his relationship with God, or his devotion to God; his pleasing God speaks of the *behavior* that arose from that relationship."[12]

Don't miss it; pleasing God is a behavior that manifests from our relationship with Him. If we are going to draw near to God so that He can draw near to us we must take a look at our behavior. Are we doing the things that please Him? You may be

---

[11] P. 15, Jerry Bridges, The Practice of Godliness, © 1983, 1996, 2008, NavPress, P.O. Box 35001, Colorado Springs, CO 80935

[12] P. 19, Jerry Bridges, The Practice of Godliness, © 1983, 1996, 2008, NavPress, P.O. Box 35001, Colorado Springs, CO 80935

doing good things but are you doing what He wants you to do? Have we disciplined ourselves to have quality time with the Father on a daily basis? If Enoch could please God, so can we. If Enoch sought God daily, so can we.

THE GOD-PLEASING FAITH

As the author of Hebrews uses Enoch as that prime example of one who pleased God, he also gave us a formula on how to please God. He says, "For he that cometh to God must believe that He is and that He is a rewarder of them that diligently seek Him" (Hebrews 11:6).

1. Coming to God
2. Diligently Seeking Him

Here is the God-pleasing behavior that God is looking for. It's a drawing-near-to-Him behavior. First, God pleasing faith looks like someone "coming to God" and someone "diligently seeking Him."

To *come to God* or *draw near to God* was another way of saying, "worship." One who came to God was a worshiper. Yeshua said that the Father seeks worshipers (John 4:23) and for those who will be sincere (in spirit) and honest (in truth) when they worship (John 4:24). We have reduced worship to a song. Worship extends further than that. Worship should always be looked upon as "I'm coming to meet with you, Yeshua, with a sincere and honest heart." When the Lord saved you, He saw a worshiper in you. He saw in you a person who could please Him. The one coming to God must seek to please Him. A true worshiper is a person who is determined to please God.

THE MEANING OF WORSHIP

The most common word for "worship" in the New Testament is *"proskyneō."* It means *"to kiss, like a dog licking his master's hand."* What a way to define worship! Now, dog lovers will enjoy this definition of worship because they can identify with their pet dog and how it will lick their hand (and face). If you've ever owned a dog as a pet, then you know very well that the dog is fully aware of whom his master is. He can pick his master out of a crowd. He knows his master's scent and loves being in his master's presence.

Favor, the affectionate name of our dog, knew the very sound of my cars' engine. Every day he could not wait for us to come home. He could hear our car turning into the neighborhood from afar. He could sense us from a great distance. He would get all excited, jumping up and down, barking, and wagging his tail and sometimes running round in circles when he knew we were arriving home. It wasn't an "Oh, okay, you're home," lazy attitude. It was pandemonium every time. We could hear him scratching at the front door in anticipation of our entrance. As soon as we turned the doorknob and entered the house, we were greeted with the grandest of welcomes. As we sat down in the great room, Favor would sit with us and begin licking away at the hand.

The Father is looking for believers who will be like Favor. He's looking for someone who can sense Him coming from afar; someone happily anticipating His entrance and longing for His presence. He's looking for someone who will express a high level of excitement every time they sense His nearness; someone who doesn't mind bowing in reverence to Him. He's looking for the dogs that lick their master's hand in reverence of Him. If a dog is man's best friend, just imagine who the Father's best friend is– the worshiper.

WE MUST BELIEVE THAT HE IS

The worshiper *"must believe that He is."* What does that mean? It doesn't just mean that we believe He exists. Many people say they believe in the existence of a God out there – a man upstairs, a higher power. It has to mean more than believing God exists. The worshiper *must be convinced* that when he approaches God that He is who He says He is – the one and only true God, the great I Am, the All-sufficient, All-knowing, Creator of all things and Father of light. The worshiper must not go through mere mechanical rituals, but he *must fully trust* that he is interacting with the true and living God. There is no need to gather in church and "worship" if we don't believe we will interact with Yeshua Himself. Every time we pray, every time we sing, praise, give, etc. it should be with the intent of meeting with God and *expecting* His interaction and have intimate encounters with Him. This kind of coming-to-God faith pleases God. This causes Him to draw near to us.

Chapter Nine - Diligently Seek Him

Revival requires that believers trust that God Himself will meet with them and do something on their behalf. He is a *rewarder*. He will reward us with His very presence. The person that is praying to God for revival must believe that Almighty God will come and do wonders in the midst of them; that He will reward them with salvation, deliverance, healings, miracles and blessings, etc.

DILIGENT SEEKERS

He only rewards diligent seekers. First of all, the Lord promised, "And ye shall seek Me and FIND Me when you seek Me with all your heart" (Jeremiah 29:13). The Lord promises that we can "find" Him. I have good news – the Lord wants to be found!

I remember as a little child one of the fun games we played. It was called, "Hide and Go Seek." In this game, everyone would hide while one person would turn their back, close their eyes and count slowly to 10 (1 Mississippi, 2 Mississippi, 3 Mississippi and so on). When the count reached 10, the counter would begin seeking after all those hidden friends in hopes of finding them without allowing them to return undetected to home base. When this game was played outdoors it was more difficult to find everyone. Some who were elected to count and seek would quit in frustration of not finding anyone. They just didn't have it in them to search persistently until they found someone. They were not "diligent" in their seeking efforts. But the ones who were diligent were relentless and determined to find at least one person. Of course, as children, we would tease the ones who couldn't find us or who quit out of frustration. The ones who refused to be teased knew what they had to do; they had to search all day if that's what it took to find someone.

The diligent seeker is a worshiper who is relentless and determined to find God no matter how long it takes. He doesn't want to be labeled as a quitter or teased because He couldn't find God. He may get frustrated at times but he will not quit until he finds Him. For revival, you must be relentless in your pursuit after God. Now that He has awakened you and made you aware of His desire, you must seek Him wholeheartedly and relentlessly. The Father rewards worshipers who have a relentless pursuit of Him.

We think that God is good at hiding, but He's not. He's only hard to find when we don't seek Him with our whole heart. He cannot deny Himself. He said that if you seek Him with your whole heart you *will* find Him (Jeremiah 29:13). Say this to yourself, "The Lord can be found and I will find Him when I seek Him with my whole heart." Diligent seekers seek God wholeheartedly and this pleases God. He will reward you with peace (Proverbs 16:7) and with whatsoever you ask of Him (1 John 3:22).

GOD SEEKERS

The book of Second Chronicles records several instances of kings who earnestly sought the Lord and how the Lord rewarded them. We can start with King Asa, how he commanded a

Chapter Nine - Diligently Seek Him

reformation in the land by taking away all the altars built for strange gods, and the high places, images, and groves. He commanded Judah to seek the Yahweh Elohim (Lord God). By seeking God, he was granted peace; he and the people who sought God with him prospered (2 Chronicles 14:1-7). King Jehoshaphat sought after God and he was blessed with riches and honor in abundance; the people of Judah constantly brought him gifts (2 Chronicles 17:3-5). As long as King Uzziah sought after God, God made him to prosper (2 Chronicles 26:5). King Hezekiah prayed for a great multitude of people that "prepared their hearts to seek God," and the Lord answered his prayer and healed the people (2 Chronicles 30:18-20). The Lord is a rewarder of them that diligently seek Him!

King David was the epitome of a God-seeker (Psalms 27:8; 63:1-2). Whether in the city near the makeshift tabernacle, or bringing home the Ark of the Covenant from the hands of the Philistines, or in the wilderness hiding from the deadly hands of King Saul, David relentlessly pursued the presence of Yahweh. He knew a secret; twice he states that Yahweh looks down upon the children of men to see if anyone was seeking Him (Psalms 14:2; 53:2). He also knew God rewards diligent seekers, "They that seek the Lord shall not lack any good thing" (Psalm 34:10). He says that those who seek Him with their whole heart are blessed (Psalm 119:2).

You can be an igniter of revival when you seek God diligently and with your whole heart. Be the seeker and the worshiper that the Father will see as He looks down upon the children of men. He will come where you are and show Himself strong on your behalf. Hold Him to His promises and take Him at His word. He is who He says He is!

Chapter Ten

Cry Out!

The Lord is not only looking for actions and behaviors, but He has His ears inclined to hear *a distinct sound* coming from the earth. Our God is a lover of sound. When He created us, He gave us the ability to make certain sounds that will cause Him to respond in favor. These sounds are released from the depths of our spirit. In the next two chapters I will reveal the kind of distinct sounds that must be made for revival to happen. These sounds must reverberate; they must be consistent.

The first of these distinct sounds that must be made for revival to happen is a *cry*. To cry out to God was a sound of desperation – it was an intense call for help.

Dr. Charles Stanley of In Touch Ministries, Inc. has this to say about crying out to God,

"In the Bible, *crying out* refers to speaking audibly with great emotion concerning an urgent need. God invites us to use this form of prayer to communicate that we *desperately need* His mercy."[13]

Pastor William McDowell, in his book, It's Happening, talks about nine postures the Lord revealed to Him in the early days of His movement. One of these postures he labeled as the posture of "Desperation." He makes the following quote about the posture of desperation:

"The posture of divine desperation leads you to a fuller awareness of your need for God. This desperation comes from God. He places longings, and sometimes circumstances or situations, in our lives that cause us to seek Him."[14]

In the proceeding chapter he shares about "the desperate cry."

"Desperation has a sound attached to it and is not quiet. This [the desperate cry] is a cry that recognizes

---

[13] https://www.crosswalk.com/devotionals/in-touch/in-touch-july-14-2011.html

[14] p. 25, William McDowell, It's Happening (A Generation is Crying Out, and Heaven is Responding), Charisma House, 600 Rinehart Road, Lake Mary, Florida 32746, ©2018

Chapter Ten - Cry Out!

that when Jesus is coming near, that is not the time to be quiet because no one else can do for you what He can."[15]

DELIVERANCE THROUGH A DESPERATE CRY

The Bible tells us the story of the Israelites in bondage in Egypt for centuries. Then there was a Pharaoh who oppressed them even the more, being paranoid by their population growth and how mighty they had become. He set taskmasters over them to afflict them and caused them to serve rigorously (Exodus 1). The labor was so severe that their lives were bitterly miserable (Exodus 1:14).

As time went on, this Pharaoh that oppressed them died. Upon his death, the children of Israel began to release a desperate cry.

"And it came to pass in the process of time that the king of Egypt died: and the children of Israel sighed by reason of the bondage, and they cried, and <u>their cry came up unto God</u> by reason of the bondage" (Exodus 2:23).

This passage of Scripture reveals what started the process of their deliverance. They approached God with their cry. It was as though God would not move on their behalf until He heard this distinct sound from them. He saw what they were

---

[15] p. 40, William McDowell, It's Happening (A Generation is Crying Out, and Heaven is Responding), Charisma House, 600 Rinehart Road, Lake Mary, Florida 32746, ©2018

going through for centuries but did nothing. He didn't invite Moses to the Burning Bush until he heard this distinct sound.

"*And the Lord said, I have surely seen the affliction of My people which are in Egypt, and <u>have heard their cry</u> by reason of their taskmasters; for I know their sorrows; and I am come down to deliver them*" (Exodus 3:7, 8).

They drew near to God with a cry and once He heard it He came down to deliver them. Had He not heard their desperate cry, Moses may have been a mere herder of Jethro's sheep. I wonder how many prophets and deliverers are waiting on the cry of the church. A desperate cry is the sound of revival. The Hebrew word for cry is *"tsâ'aqah"* which means *"to call for help; to cry out in need."* The Israelite captives knew that Yahweh was the only one who could help them in their time of need. Their cry intensified to a groaning (*ne'âqah* - Exodus 2:24). Brown-Driver-Briggs defines *ne'âqah* as a cry that denotes *heavy affliction*. Can you imagine the heavy sound that was stirred among the captives? Their oppressors had to have heard it too. It was loud and intense. The level of their cry to God superseded the level of their pain and bondage.

WHEN RAVENS CRY

The Greek Septuagint parallels tsâ'aqah with *krazo* which literally means *"to croak like a raven."* Smith's Bible Dictionary says that the smell of death is so gratifying to the raven that

Chapter Ten - Cry Out!

when passing over sheep and a tainted smell is detected, the raven begins to cry very loudly.[16] In other words, the nearer it gets to its prey, the raven croaks louder as it zeroes in on the opportunity to satisfy its hunger.

Israel sensed an opportunity for freedom upon the tainted smell of Pharaoh's death. It was like the light bulb was turned on in their minds of the greatest opportunity to reach God. It was time to cry out to God like never before. They didn't keep quiet as they became aware that no one could do what they needed done for them but Yahweh. They saw the magnitude of their need for Him and began to cry out with a ravenous sound and wouldn't stop until their deliverance was complete. Revival broke out in Egypt! Steven Hovater made a simple but powerful statement in his sermon. Cry Out – Exodus 2:23-25 about the cry. He says, *"Crying out is waking up!"*[17] King David quotes, "The righteous cry out, and the Lord hears" (Psalm 34:17) and "His ears are open to their cry" (Psalm 34:15).

God is said to "hear" the prayers which He accepts and grants and to be "deaf" to those which He does not grant but rejects. Israel cried out to Yahweh for help and he heard, accepted and granted their petition. Their cry was effective and fervent (James 5:16). God heard their desperate, raven-like cry

---

[16] Smith, William, Dr. Entry for "Raven." Smith's Bible Dictionary. www.studylight.org/dic/sbd/view.cgi?number=T3599. 1901

[17] http://stevenhovater.com/cry-out-a-sermon-from-exodus-223-25/

and did three things in response to their cry that led to a mighty deliverance from their oppression:

1. He remembered His covenant
2. He looked upon the children of Israel and
3. He had respect unto them

HE REMEBERED HIS COVENANT

Yahweh had established an everlasting covenant with Abraham that we benefit from today (Genesis 12:1-3; 15:5-6, 12-14; 17:5-8). Through faith in Messiah, Yeshua (Jesus Christ), we are sons of God and the seed of Abraham and heirs according to the promise (Galatians 3:26-29) and are blessed with faithful Abraham (Galatians 3:9).

God *remembered* His covenant. God is not forgetful or scatter-brained; He knows all things. I don't want to appear so theological, but Moses is said to be speaking anthropomorphically here. This means that he was attributing a human characteristic here to express what God was doing in response to hearing their cry. I believe Yahweh had refused to acknowledge them while they were complacent and content in their bondage. When He heard their cry, it was a sign that they were discontent with their condition. This caused Yahweh to remove His stance of refusal toward them. It was their cry that caused Him to acknowledge the agreement that He made with Abraham.

Chapter Ten - Cry Out!

The Lord takes the same stance with us who are also the seed of Abraham through faith in Yeshua. If we are complacent and content with our present condition then He lets us be. The moment we start crying out to Him in discontent – and for His help – He will begin to acknowledge His agreement that He made with Abraham and the very act of redemption made on that rugged cross on Calvary's mountain through the shed blood of His Son, Yeshua.

HE LOOKED UPON THE CHILDREN OF ISRAEL

Yahweh *looked upon* them. The Hebrew word *"râ'âh"* is used here and it means *"to look intently at."* The Lord heard their cry and studied how He would answer them. Not all revivals are alike. God answers every cry based upon the specificity of needs. Revival is not merely about the Lord performing miracles. It is more about Him fulfilling specific needs of those who are crying out to Him for help even if it takes miracles to meet those needs. There were different needs met at the Wales Revival than at the Azusa Street Revival or at the Brownsville Revival. What the Lord did for Moses and the Israelites in Egypt was different for what He did during the time of Yochanan and Yeshua. He parted the Jordan River for Joshua, but He kept the river banks flowing for Yochanan to baptize people unto repentance. Yahweh assesses the needs of the people who are crying out for Him. In some revivals you may see blind eyes open and deaf ears hearing, while in others you may see people getting out of wheelchairs and demons cast out of people. The cry is released because of specific needs you desire God to meet. You want Him to look intently at your situation so the He can answer your need precisely.

HE HAD RESPECT UNTO THEM

The Lord heard and accepted their deep cry for help, acknowledged His eternal agreement with them, looked intently at their situation and assessed their need. Lastly, He *"had respect unto them."* This meant that He *favored* them. He favored them by personally intervening and doing for them what they could not do on their own. There was no earthly way possible for them to get out of the bondage they were in. It had to take God's supernatural power to work on their behalf. It was a mighty deliverance whereby God parted the Red Sea and drowned Pharaoh's great army and approximately 2 million people – men, women and children – were freed from slavery and not one feeble (weak or unhealthy) among them. Revival! We know that slavery can take a toll on a person's physical and mental health. In this instance of deliverance, before their exodus, God's miraculous power swept through Israel's slave quarters and healed them all. There was not a Hebrew who couldn't make it across the Red Sea.

The great thing about revival is that most of us find ourselves in situations and conditions in which we cannot get out of by our own human strength; it will take the hand of God to move on our behalf. Your cry says, "I trust in the miracle working power of the Most High God." For those whom

Chapter Ten - Cry Out!

Yahweh has awakened and are praying fervently for God to come where you are, you are crying out for God to move upon your life, church, and city with His miracle working power to do something that cannot be done by human capabilities of anyone in that region. The Lord will hear your cry and favor you where there will be no needs gone unmet.

WE CRY ABBA, FATHER

We have the Spirit of Revival in us. It is He who awakens us from our spiritual apathy and puts a sense of urgency in our spirit to cry out to the Father for Him to come where we are and meet our needs. He will stir us to cry out for the presence of God and His miracle working power.

"For you did not receive the spirit of bondage again to fear, but you received the Spirit of adoption by whom we <u>cry out</u>, Abba, Father" (Romans 8:15).

"Likewise the Spirit also helps in our weaknesses. For we do not know what we should pray for as we ought, but the Spirit Himself makes intercession for us with <u>groanings</u> which cannot be uttered" (Romans 8:26).

"And because you are sons, God has sent forth the Spirit of His Son into your hearts, <u>crying out</u>, 'Abba, Father!'" (Galatians 4:6)

Spirit-filled believers have been given an encoded prayer language that the enemy cannot decode. When I'm at the point of not knowing how to verbalize what I'm sensing, the Spirit of

God within me will begin to make inarticulate sounds that I release (Romans 8:26). The New American Standard Bible translates these groaning sounds to be "too deep for words." It's that deep calling unto deep that I mentioned earlier.

These groaning sounds are what the Father identifies with. He locates people on the earth who are releasing these groaning sounds and looks intently upon their need to favor them. The Father searches the hearts of men and interprets the Spirit's intercession for us (Romans 8:27). He knows exactly what these sounds are. They are the sounds of the Spirit. They are the words of the Holy Spirit encoded only for His ears. They are distinct sounds that He is pleased with. It is the sound of someone who is putting their trust in Him.

These groaning sounds are the Spirit's intercession for our *"weaknesses."* Dutch Sheets defines this word *"weakness (Gk. Asthenia)"* as *"an inability to produce results."*[18] The Spirit is helping us in our human limitation. He communicates to the Father what we are incapable of discerning at certain times. Sometimes we cannot discern what we really need or how to convey it to God, but the Spirit knows and relays it to the Father. This is why the apostle Jude encouraged us to "pray in the Holy Ghost" (Jude 1:20).

These sounds will eventually bring the comforting power of our heavenly Father to us. He will answer us in power. There is a deep cry in your heart that must be released. Allow the Holy

---

[18] p. 97, Intercessory Prayer, Dutch Sheets, Regal Books, Ventura, California, USA © 1996

Chapter Ten - Cry Out!

Spirit to make distinctive sounds within you that are too deep for human words and watch the Lord respond in His miraculous power for you and the needs of those around you. Revival starts with you releasing a ravenous cry to the Lord.

Chapter Eleven

The Sound that Pleases God

There is another sound that the Father delights in that causes Him to respond in favor to His children. It is the sound that draws Him close to us. We refer to this sound as *praise*. Praise is expressive. It initiates from the heart and manifests itself outwardly in different bodily expressions. I haven't found anywhere in the Word of God where praise was merely an inward celebration. Every mentioning of praise resulted in outward, visible expressions from the worshiper. Praise is not quiet.

THE PRAISE PROBLEM

We often hear excuses such as being shy or introverted from people who aren't expressive when it comes to praise. Sadly, many pastors may not challenge the unexpressive worshiper to release the praises that are due unto Him. Worship leaders have grown immune to non-praising believers sitting in the midst of the congregation. Sure, there will be people who outwardly praise Yeshua but are not sincere. Yeshua, too, was aware of this when He said, "This people draweth nigh unto Me with their mouth, and honoureth Me with their lips; but their heart is far from Me" (Matthew 15:8). We will let Yeshua judge their praise. However, insincere people praising God do not change the fact that praise is still an outward expression. You may not agree with me but God created everyone with the ability to openly express how worthy He is to them. Not only does the Lord desire our praise but he deserves our praise. "Let *every thing that hath breath* praise the Lord. Praise ye the Lord" (Psalm 150:6). If you have breath you can praise the Lord.

The church has not mastered praise, at least the kind that brings revival. Have you noticed an increase in worship songs (and artists) but asked yourself why does revival tarry if we are releasing a sound the Lord delights in? Here are a few reasons why revival tarries:

Chapter Eleven - The Sound that Pleases God

1. We haven't incorporated praise into our daily personal time of devotion.
2. We have reduced praise to Sunday morning worship.
3. We have undealt with sin in the heart (Psalm 66:18).
4. We live selfishly and our relationship with the Lord is not our number one priority.
5. We've been taught that praising God outwardly is emotionalism.
6. We have too much fear of what someone will say about us "acting undignified." They say, "It doesn't take all that." In return, you don't want to feel "embarrassed."
7. We have too much disunity and discord in the local church.
8. We have worship leaders, teams and musicians who aren't living wholeheartedly for God.

SIN HAS A SOUND

Sin has a sound that distorts the sound of revival. Sound experts would call it interference. The waveform of sin interferes with the sound of revival ultimately silences it. The sound of murmur and complaining caused many to die in the wilderness. There are other evil sounds such as backbiting, profanity, lying, bearing false witness and gossip that interferes with and disturbs the sound of revival.

Gamblers have the sound of when slot machine levers are pulled, Black Jack dealers shuffling cards, dices rolled against Craps tables or from the little ball jumping around on the Roulette wheel. Murder has a sound of gunshots. Fornication, adultery and illicit sex have sounds of sexual noises in defiled bedrooms. The drunkard pouring his whiskey into the glass makes a sound. Opioids have a sound of when caps are taken off pill bottles or flames being lit to cook cocaine. Night clubs and reveling has the sound of worldly music being played.

Would you believe me if I told you these sounds are in the church? We physically hear the worship team singing and musicians playing, but in the spirit realm the sound of sin reverberates from the lives of unawaken, unrepentant, lukewarm believers.

It interferes with the sound of revival and you, who are awakened and sensitive to the Spirit, must confront it with the word of God, fasting and fervent prayers. The Lord will begin to bring people to a place of repentance so that these sounds of sin will dissipate and revival can ignite.

THE SOUND THAT PLEASES GOD

There is a sound that pleases God. It's the sound of revival. The sound of prophets prophesying, broken hearts crying out to Abba, prayer warriors offering up daily prayers, shofars blowing, worshipers worshiping, believers confessing His word and sinners repenting. Revival is the sound that pleases God.

Chapter Eleven - The Sound that Pleases God

We hear the sound of crutches falling to the floor and wheelchairs being folded while the footsteps of the lame walk across sanctuary floors. We hear the sound of the mute talking for the very first time, the deaf and blind rejoicing from receiving their miracle and the giving of thanks from families whose needs are fulfilled by the giving of the saints. This pleases God.

In the spirit realm we can hear the voice of cherubim singing, "Holy, holy, holy is the Lord God Almighty," and the wings of messenger angels moving swiftly as they ascend and descend delivering revelations and creative miracles to the church. We hear ancient doors opening, walls of strongholds flattening, the trembling of demons, holy angels rejoicing over sinners coming to Christ, and the wind whistling from the rolling back of the heavens as they open over us. This pleases our Father!

THE SOUND OF PRAISE

The Lord is a lover of praise. Praise is multifaceted and multidimensional. There are several ways that we can express ourselves in adoration to God. Many believers are aware that the original Hebrew language uses at least seven words for praise. There are a few more words that are closely related to praise that I will include in this discussion. Each of these words give us a clue of the kind of sound that the Lord delights in and are necessary for the heavens to open over you personally, over your church corporately, and over your region.

There are vocal and non-vocal praise expressions. The vocal praises are the *rûa, rananah, todah, yadah, tehillah* and *shabach*. The non-vocal praises are the *barak, zamar, taqa* and *machol*. The non-vocal praises usually accommodates the vocal praises. However, they all are expressive and move the heart of God.

THE VOCAL PRAISES

1. <u>The *Rûa'* Praise</u>. In Psalm 100 we find the phrase "joyful noise" as the translation of rûa'. The actual definition of this word is "to shout or to raise a sound; to shout a war-cry; alarm." A prime example of this rûa' is found in Joshua 6. In order for the Israelites to take possession of the land God had promised them they had to conquer those who were already occupying it. The first city they came upon was the city of Jericho. Jericho was known as an impenetrable stronghold. The inhabitants had fortified themselves against all resisting forces.

To conquer Jericho, Israel could not do it their way, they had to rely on Yahweh. Yahweh told Joshua to march around the stronghold of Jericho once every day for six days and then seven times on the seventh day. On the first six days they did nothing but march. They were not instructed to build a catapult to hurl fiery boulders at the walls nor could they prepare arrows to lunge across the walls to strike the inhabitants – just marching in silence until they were instructed to release a rûa' after the sounding of the trumpet (shofar) blasts (Joshua 6:10).

Chapter Eleven - The Sound that Pleases God

As the very last footstep marched around Jericho seven times 'round, Joshua instructed the priests to blow the trumpets. Then he instructed the people to "rûa with a *great* rûa." When the people of God released the great shout, the thick, impenetrable walls of Jericho fell down flat before their eyes (Joshua 6:20). When the people shouted, God moved miraculously on their behalf. Your shout can open the heavens! Your shout can summon God's supernatural power. Your shout is a *warfare* praise. It's a spiritual weapon given to us by God to demolish strongholds (2 Corinthians 10:4).

There are demons that have built strongholds over your life and have been there in your family's history. There are principalities who govern your region barricaded behind certain laws, doctrines, belief systems and social tolerances. Your responsibility as an awakened believer expecting revival is to lead the people of God into a great shout that will flatten these strongholds. Get your shout back! Demons tremble when they hear the deafening alarm of a great rûa coming from the encampment of God's people! Get your vocal chords ready because it's time to release a rûa for your region.

2. <u>The *Renânâh* Praise</u>. We are instructed to "come before His presence with *singing*" (Psalm 100:2). This is another way of drawing near to God so that He will draw near to us. If we want God to come to where we are then we must release the renânâh praise. The renânâh praise shows Yahweh that we desire His presence. Renânâh is defined as "a ringing cry or a shout for joy." It is derived from the word *rânan* meaning *"to overcome."*

So renânâh can be looked at in two unique ways. First, it can be seen as joyful outbursts of those who triumph in battles.

Renânâh is usually a song of victory. I like to parallel it to sporting events where the team who scores a goal, they and their fans, break out in cheers and songs of joy happily convinced that they are going to win or have just won the game. It's pandemonium in the stadium. If you've ever gone to a sporting event like football or soccer then you know exactly what I'm talking about. The church falls way behind in our cheering for victory. We must start winning more significant battles if we want to release that ringing outburst of joy. We need to take a good look at some of the difficulties we are facing today and with confidence know that the Lord will always cause us to triumph in His name. Should I remind you that you're on the winning team? You have all you need to be triumphant in battles, to overcome temptations and trials. Overcome so you can make a ringing sound of joy unto the Lord.

Secondly, renânâh can be understood as being so overwhelmed with joy because you are approaching the presence of God that you burst aloud with repeated singing. There's no greater feeling than anticipating the presence of the Lord and being confident that He will meet you where you are. "But let all those that put their trust in thee rejoice: let them ever *shout for joy* (renânâh), because thou defendest them: let them also that love thy name be joyful in thee" (Psalm 5:11).

3. <u>The *Todah* and *Yadah* Praises</u>. *Todah* means to give thanks to God. It's a praise of gratitude. It is lifting up your

Chapter Eleven - The Sound that Pleases God

voice in appreciation for what the Lord has done for you. There are many things that Yahweh has done for us. Spiritually, He has shown us mercy, provided redemption by the sacrifice of His only begotten son, Yeshua, opened up doors for us that no man can shut, given us wisdom and understanding, and protects us from the hand of the enemy. Physically, He has blessed us with health and a roof over our heads. "I have been young and now am old; yet have I not seen the righteous forsaken, nor his seed begging bread" (Psalm 37:25).

I remember watching the TV Show, The Four, where new artist are in a contest to be the next singing sensation. Familiar music producers such as Sean Combs aka "P-Diddy," and DJ Khaled are among the celebrity judges. While encouraging one of the contestants, I remember DJ Khaled making this statement: "If you're gonna be great, you have to be grateful." That stuck with me. If we're going to be great in God, we have to be grateful for what He has done for us and for our relationship with Him. If we're going to be great we must consistently give God a todah praise.

Speaking of greatness, the Hebrews sometimes use a similar word to todah. This word is *yadah*. Yadah is also a praise of thanksgiving but with extended hands. Yadah is derived from Yehudah (Judah). The name, Judah, also means praise. The prophecy over Judah was that he was going to be lion-like. Judah's blessing included victory over his enemies, rulership of the nation, prosperity for Judah's descendants, and that from his descendants Messiah would come (Genesis 49:8-

10). In fact, the Messiah is called the Lion of the tribe of Judah (Revelation 5:5). How's that for greatness!

I say, yadah praise comes from people who have potential to be great. When you're extending your hands in worship while giving thanks to God, it's only preparing you to have the attitude of being great in Him.

Remember, we can *"enter His gates"* or draw near to God with a *todah* praise – a praise of thanksgiving (Psalm 100:4). You're not just making noise, but you're drawing near to God with the intention of Him drawing near to you or coming to where you are

4. <u>The *Tehillah* (and *Hallal*) Praise</u>. We also can "enter into His courts with *tehillah*" (Psalm 100:4). Tehillah means "to celebrate; to *be boastful* usually with singing." We are to sing songs which boast about the goodness of God, which speaks of His awesome character. King David said, "…His praise (tehillah) shall continually be in my mouth" (Psalm 34:1), He is "enthroned upon the praise (tehillah) of His people" (Psalm 22:3), and "praise (tehillah) is comely for the upright (Psalm 33:1). Our continual, frequent celebrating and boasting about our God pleases Him and causes Him to sit among us. When He shows up to our praise festival anything can happen!

5. <u>The *Shabach* Praise</u>. *Shabach* means, *"to shout, to address in a loud tone, to command, to triumph."* "O clap your hands, all ye people; shout *(shabach)* unto God with the voice of triumph" (Psalm 47:1) and "Cry out and shout *(shabach),* thou inhabitant

Chapter Eleven - The Sound that Pleases God

of Zion: for great is the Holy One of Israel in the midst of thee" (Isaiah 12:6). Again, we see another word for praise that is interpreted as "a shout." We must get used to making loud intentional noises to our God if we want Him to show up. I've heard prominent preachers say, "You don't have to do all that shouting and screaming because God is not deaf." Well, according to several Hebrew words for praise, I beg to differ. It seems like if we want His attention, we need to be loud and demonstrative.

THE NON-VOCAL PRAISES

1. The *Barak* Praise. This is a kneeling down before Him in deep adoration of who He is. It's the posture that signifies our submission and yielding to God. You don't necessarily have to say anything, but kneel in humble adoration as though you are before His throne and are awestruck of His person, His presence, His provision, and His loving care for you. "I will bless *(barak)* the Lord at all times..." (Psalm 34:1). "O come let us worship and bow down; let us kneel *(barak)* before the Lord our maker" (Ps 95:6). Admittedly, we rarely see this kind of praise going on today. Usually, when we are praising God in our worship services, worshipers are standing. It may not be a new song the Lord is looking for, but more kneeling in adoration with the songs we're already singing. "Humble yourselves therefore under the mighty hand of God, that He may exalt you in due time" (1 Peter 5:6). Our kneeling may take us to a higher level of worship.

The prophet Daniel is a good example of one who blessed (barak) the Lord at all times. The Bible makes record of Daniel kneeling (barak) in prayer and giving thanks (yadah) to God three times a day consistently (Daniel 6:10). He did this even in the face of danger when there was an edict from King Darius disallowing any man to pray to any God, for thirty days, except the king. Daniel refused to comply with the decree and prayed and praised Yahweh like he normally would do every day. Eventually, he was arrested and thrown into the lions' den. But the Lord sent an angel and shut the mouths of the lions so that they would not hurt him (Daniel 6:22). Great deliverance and miracles can happen for those who kneel daily in adoration of our God!

2. The *Zamar* Praise. Zamar is simply the sounding of instruments that accommodate the worship. It is worship music. It is praising God with instruments.

3. The *Taqa* Praise. The clapping of hands also accommodated the boastful singing and praises of God's people. We see again in Psalm 47:1 where clapping was used with shouting. "O *clap (taqa)* your hands, all ye people; shout (shabach) unto God with the voice of triumph" (Psalm 47:1). We can praise God with our hands.

4. The *Mechōlâh (machol)* Praise. Not only can we praise God with our hands, we can praise Him with our feet. Mechōlâh is dancing. Our feet make sounds of praise. Express

Chapter Eleven - The Sound that Pleases God

is worthiness with your feet. Dancing was the norm among the Hebrews as they celebrated Yahweh.

When Israel crossed the Red Sea, Moses sang a song of victory, then his sister, Miriam, and all the Hebrew women grabbed tambourines and began to *dance* and sing to the Lord (Exodus 15:20, 21). When David returned from defeating Goliath and the Philistines, the Hebrew women from every city came out to celebrate with him and the army of Israel. They sang songs, played musical instruments and *danced* (1 Samuel 18:6, 21:11, 29:5). King David, when bringing the Ark of the Covenant back to Israel, also *danced before the Lord*. He *wildly danced* out of his linen ephod (2 Samuel 6:14-16). "Let them praise His name in the *dance (machol):* let them sing praises unto Him with the timbrel and harp" (Psalm 149:3). When the prodigal son returned home, the father celebrated with a feast and the elder brother coming from out of the field heard music and dancing as he drew near to the house (Luke 15:25).

The Lord loves to hear the sound of dancing. He wants us to praise Him with our entire being. Praise Him with a sincere heart, praise Him with your mouth, praise Him with your hands and feet and praise Him with instruments. Praise Him in song, with music, with hand claps, with raised hands, with uplifted, extended hands and kneeling in adoration. Praise Him loudly, boisterously, triumphantly, and with a great shout! When we celebrate Him and give thanks to Him consistently, He will come and inhabit our praise and do great and mighty things. Authentic, heartfelt, expressive praise is the distinct sound that the Lord is willing to open the heavens for and draw near to His people in power and glory.

Chapter Twelve

Fulfilling the Burden of Revival

Do you sense the burden of Revival? Have you been awakened to God's desire to come where you are? Do you feel burdened to cry out for the Lord to change your city? Do you feel the desperate need for His presence and nearness for yourself and your church? Are you willing to make the appropriate sacrifices to see God move in the midst of His people? Will you dedicate your life to a life of fellowship with God until you see Revival come? If this is you, here are a few things you can do now to meet your burden for God to come where you are:

PERSONAL REVIVAL PREPARATIONS

1. Make sure your heart is right with God through repentance.
2. Examine your faith for lukewarmness and pray for a burning passion for God.
3. Make sure you don't have any unforgiveness or resentment against anyone.
4. Make quality time for prayer and cry out to God for Revival. Make a daily appointment with God and keep it!
5. Engulf yourself in the word of God.
6. Study books on revival and research past and present revivals.
7. Schedule days of fasting for personal growth.
8. Guard your "gates." Faith comes by hearing (Romans 10:17). Refuse to listen to and entertain ungodly conversations and music. Watch what you look at on television, movies, etc., and be careful what you say out of your mouth (it can defile you) (Matthew 15:18-20).
9. Make a daily proclamation that the heavens are open over you.
10. Praise the Lord with more intensity; worship more freely.

11. Never despise the day of small beginnings. God will do what He promised. He will come.

CHURCH AND CITYWIDE REVIVAL PREPARATIONS

1. Meet with your pastor and share with him the burden you have for Revival.
2. Link your church with national prayer groups. For example, our church linked up with IHOP (International House of Prayer) and started a "House of Prayer" here in Odenton, Maryland. We also pray alongside other "Houses of Prayer" in the Delmarva-DC region. We are expecting regional revival, so it will take more than just us. Our goal is to have a 24-hour prayer center established. You must start from somewhere.
3. We were encouraged to set the atmosphere in our church by playing worship music 24/7 in the sanctuary. There's not a moment where God does not hear worship permeating from our sanctuary.
4. Establish times of prayer with your church. Prayer warriors come together on Monday nights for prayer to bombard heaven. We also have the church open and available for anyone to come pray during the day, every day.
5. Talk to your pastor about periods of fasting with the church specifically for Revival. Our church fasts together every Tuesday.
6. Pray for your worship leader and speak often to them

about Revival. Perhaps get a copy of this book into the hands of the worship team in hopes of spiritual awakening.
7. Pray specifically for local pastors, city officials and others in seats of authority.
8. Make sure that you are a giver. You must support and sow into the Revival that you are expecting.

TEN CHARACTERISTICS OF REVIVALS

Each revival or awakening leaves its own heat signature; in 1740 youth led the way, in 1857 businessmen and prayer took center stage, and the 1906 Azusa Street revival was decidedly interracial. Yet all share common themes. What are the most frequently mentioned characteristics of revivals and awakenings in literature?

1. **TIMING**: Revivals emerge during times of spiritual and moral decline, which leads to intense prayer.
2. **PRAYER**: God puts a longing into the hearts of many to pray for revival.
3. **THE WORD**: The preaching or reading of God's Word brings deep conviction and desire for Christ.
4. **THE HOLY SPIRIT**: The Holy Spirit takes people to a spiritual depth they could not achieve on their own.
5. **CONVICTION**: Affected sinners are inconsolable except in Christ.
6. **GLORY FOR GOD**: God receives praise, honor, and

glory for bringing revival.

7. **REFORMATION AND RENEWAL:** Revival produces lasting fruit. New ministries are founded and society experiences a reform of morals as more and more people convert.
8. **MANIFESTATIONS:** Manifestations like fainting, groaning prayer, and miracles vary by culture and denomination.
9. **MESSY:** Revivals are messy--controversies swirl about miracles, abuses, excesses, suspicions, and theological disputes (to name but a few).
10. **CYCLICAL:** Revivals inevitably crest and decline.[19]

You can be part of "the generation that seeks His face" (Psalm 24:6). The Lord has called you to His kingdom in this season to be more than just a church-goer. Your city needs you more than they ever know. You have the nature and the DNA of a revivalist. There is a cry that will come forth from you and stir the heart of God. There's a praise that you will release that will cause God to draw near to you and enthrone. You have a shout that will demolish strongholds. Unprecedented miracles await your faith. The Lord is gracious and will do something for you that you could have never done in your own strength. The

---

[19] http://patrickmorley.com/blog/2015/6/23/a-brief-history-of-spiritual-revival-and-awakening-in-america

burden of Revival is upon you and it won't relent until He has come to where you are.

Let our prayer be like that of the prophet Isaiah,

"Oh, that you would rend the heavens, that you would come down, that the mountains might shake at Your presence."

About the Author

Antonio M. Palmer is the Senior Pastor of Kingdom Celebration Center in Odenton, Maryland and Presiding Bishop of Kingdom Alliance of Churches International where he oversees 34 churches. He has been preaching the Gospel since 1993 and began his first church in 1995 where he founded "Growing in Grace Ministries" (later called The Burning Bush) in Annapolis, Maryland.

During his pastoral tenure, he has raised up Bishops, Elders, Ministers, Deacons, and ministry workers for the work of the kingdom and the furtherance of the Gospel around the world.

Bishop Palmer does extensive missionary work in several foreign countries from preaching at Crusades and Conferences to ministering humanitarian assistance to thousands of needy children. He helps with church planting and provides financial care to several orphanages in East Africa.

Bishop Palmer holds a Bachelors of Divinity and Masters in Pastoral Counseling and has been the recipient of various awards such as three Governor Citations, a County Executive Citation, and a MLK, Jr. Drum Major Award for his dedication to serving the community.

Bishop Palmer is an entrepreneur and owner of four (4) businesses: Kingdom Publishing, LLC, Kingdom Kafé and Lounge, Kingdom Kare Childcare Center, Inc., and Palm Tree Business Consulting.

In addition to this book, Bishop Palmer has authored three other life-changing books, "God's Rest Revealed" (A Life Flowing with Milk and Honey), "Building an Effective Prayer Life" and "Mark the Perfect Man."

Bishop Palmer enjoys working in ministry alongside his beautiful wife and friend, Pastor Barbara Palmer. They share bundles of laughter and life lessons with their son, Randy, their daughter-in-law, Kimberly and their adorable and playful four grandchildren – Katriel, Khairi, Rylei and Ravyn.

www.ingramcontent.com/pod-product-compliance
Lightning Source LLC
Chambersburg PA
CBHW041318110526
44591CB00021B/2832